Coa
prof   motivated
prof
                                              Practice provides a
prac   ...ess skills needed to succeed
as a   ...p..syed coach and coaching psychologist. It focuses on
every aspect of setting up and developing a professional and
successful coaching practice, including discussion of how to market
your business, manage your resources, assess risk and promote a
professional image.

Assuming no prior knowledge or experience of running a business, this book provides an invaluable guide to the major financial,
legal and practical issues involved in setting up a coaching practice.
It will be welcomed by all coaches, whatever their level of experience.

Gladeana McMahon is a leading personal development and
executive coach. She is a Vice President and Fellow of the Association
for Coaching and a Fellow of the British Association for Counselling
and Psychotherapy.

Professor Stephen Palmer PhD is a chartered psychologist, an
APECS Founding Accredited Executive Coach and APECS Founding
Accredited Supervisor of Executive Coaches. He is Honorary President
of the Association for Coaching, and in 2005 he was Chair of the
British Psychological Society Special Group in Coaching Psychology.
He is Director of the Centre for Coaching, Honorary Professor of
Psychology at City University, London and Visiting Professor of Work
Based Learning and Stress Management at NCWBLP, Middlesex
University.

Christine Wilding is a Chartered (MCIPD) human resource
practitioner, trainer and coach, with post-graduate training in
Cognitive Behavioural Therapy. Christine works in both private and
corporate sectors, both coaching individuals and training groups in
motivational and inter-personal skills.

Essential Coaching Skills and Knowledge
Series Editors: Gladeana McMahon,
Stephen Palmer & Averil Leimon

The **Essential Coaching Skills and Knowledge** series provides an accessible and lively introduction to key areas in the developing field of coaching. Each title in the series is written by leading coaches with extensive experience and has a strong practical emphasis, including illustrative vignettes, summary boxes, exercises and activities. Assuming no prior knowledge, these books will appeal to professionals in business, management, human resources, psychology, counselling and psychotherapy, as well as students and tutors of coaching and coaching psychology.

Titles in the series

Achieving Excellence in Your Coaching Practice
Gladeana McMahon, Stephen Palmer & Christine Wilding

Essential Business Coaching
Averil Leimon, Francois Moscovici & Gladeana McMahon

Achieving Excellence in Your Coaching Practice

How to run a highly successful coaching business

Gladeana McMahon,
Stephen Palmer &
Christine Wilding

Routledge
Taylor & Francis Group

LONDON AND NEW YORK

First published 2006
by Routledge
27 Church Road, Hove, East Sussex, BN3 2FA

Simultaneously published in the USA and Canada
by Routledge
270 Madison Avenue, New York, NY 10016

Routledge is an imprint of the Taylor & Francis Group

© 2006 Gladeana McMahon, Stephen Palmer & Christine Wilding

Typeset in New Century Schoolbook by
Keystroke, Jacaranda Lodge, Wolverhampton

Printed and bound in Great Britain by
Biddles Ltd, King's Lynn
Paperback cover design by Lisa Dynan

This publication has been produced with paper manufactured to strict
environmental standards and with pulp derived from sustainable forests.

British Library Cataloguing in Publication Data
A catalogue record for this book is available from the British Library

Library of Congress Cataloging in Publication Data
McMahon, Gladeana, 1954–
    Achieving excellence in your coaching practice: how to run a
highly successful coaching business / by Gladeana McMahon,
Stephen Palmer and Christine Wilding.
        p. cm.
Includes bibliographical references and index.
    ISBN 1-58391-895-7 (hbk) – ISBN 1-58391-896-5 (pbk)
1. Executive coaching. 2. Personal coaching. 3. Success in business.
I. Palmer, Stephen, 1955– II. Wilding, Christine. III. Title.
HD30.4.M436 2005
658.4'07124–dc22

                                    2005013778

                        ISBN 1–58391–895–7 (hbk)
                        ISBN 1–58391–896–5 (pbk)

                        ISSN 1749-1185

To Mike as always for his continued love and support, and to all the many practitioners whose constant questions and demands have helped me develop my knowledge of how to run a successful practice. (GM)

To my parents and family (SP)

To Chris, without whose wonderful early support and advice I would probably still be chewing the end of my pencil! (CW)

Contents

Preface

Over the last 30 years or so, life choices have proliferated. While increased options are helpful in many ways, they have also resulted in individuals becoming more uncertain about their own personal "best way forward" and how they can achieve what they want without making a catalogue of mistakes along the way. We also now have an increased awareness of the excellent results we can obtain by defining what is really important to us, and setting specific goals to achieve what we want.

"Coaching" in the past normally meant going down to the sports club for some instruction – or the sort of help we might try to purchase for a schoolchild needing to pass a particular exam. However, now that we have become more familiar with the idea of seeking solutions to life crises and personal difficulties through the purchase of professional services, it has not taken long for a wide audience to become interested in such services. Coaching as a career has developed in response.

Coaching embraces the concept of "positive psychology": instead of dragging ourselves from −10 to zero (zero being "OK"), we have become interested in how to get from zero to +10 (achieving goals and a better life). Interest in the idea of professionals who can teach the life skills and techniques to achieve this has become more widespread. Demand for coaching services, both for individuals and in corporate settings, continues to increase. Good quality coach training is more widely available.

Because coaching is only now beginning to establish itself as a profession, what is *not* yet so available is the professional guidance necessary for coaches – or those considering coaching as a career option – that will enable them to build, maintain and sustain a thriving independent coaching practice.

We have written this book in order to fill this gap: to enable you to achieve the skills and knowledge necessary both to start up and to maintain a flourishing and rewarding private practice that we hope will be both challenging and stimulating – as well as financially successful.

Introduction

Who is this book for?

We are making an initial assumption: that you are already a trained coach, currently in training or interested in becoming trained. Whatever your situation, we will provide you with the essential knowledge and skills to run your own practice. In some cases, this detailed knowledge may, in fact, lead you to decide not to go into private practice. If so, we shall still regard that as a successful outcome to our endeavours. We want you to be able to make a good, informed choice.

So this book is for those of you who are:

- Considering a freelance coaching career. We hope to offer you enough information to help you draw a sound conclusion about this.
- Already starting out as independent professionals, but who would like to professionalise their service and ensure that they develop a solid business base. Many of you may already have set up private practices, but feel you could benefit from learning about more effective ways to develop your business and increase your income.
- Experienced coaches, who may already be familiar with many of the basic strategies we discuss, but would welcome further advice on the many ways you can increase your client base and further expand your business.
- In related careers, including business consultants, who would like to develop integrated careers in which coaching is one of several skills that you offer.

It may even be that we will give you ideas and information that will cause you to reconsider the structure of your business. In any event, if you are serious about developing a flourishing practice, then this book is for you, and we feel confident that giving time to reading it will greatly enhance your business.

This book, therefore, is for anyone who genuinely wishes to work in a more professional way, increase their client base and increase their income-generating capacity.

An emphasis on skills and practice

In teaching you new business skills we are, in essence, planning to "coach the coach". We want to ensure that you have the most effective business strategies in place, and that you are carrying them out to good effect. We want to suggest new pathways that you may try, and show you how to monitor their success. We want to save you from unnecessary pitfalls, and we want to ensure that you both understand and feel confident about any changes you are making, or new areas of development that you may enter into or expand.

Your own coaching skills will serve you well – but even a coach needs a great deal of practical information at his or her fingertips in order to make a success of a very competitive area of work.

This book is practical and skills-based, rather than academic, and theoretical argument, references and discussion are kept to a minimum. We have, however, placed a bibliography and reading list at the end of the book for those who wish to pursue individual aspects in further depth.

In writing this book, we have considered the skills needed to work within the various professional areas of coaching: personal, life, corporate, speciality, executive or business performance coaching and coaching psychology. However, for ease of reference, we simply refer to "coaching" generically in the text, which we hope you will understand to include all of the above.

PART 1

Being self-employed

1

Why do you want to be self-employed?

Coaching is an exciting new career that appeals to many people. However, what we are actually talking about now is setting up and running your own business.

If you are serious about starting out on your own, you may benefit from looking at all the pros and cons, and being honest with yourself about your own personality traits and lifestyle hopes. Will all these fit well with the demands of being self-employed?

It may be that you are presently working within an organisation on an employed basis. What has made you decide: "I want to be a self-employed coach"? Such an important career/life change has the potential to bring excitement, hard work and challenge, but for some it can also trigger anxiety.

As a coach, you would no doubt be asking a client to begin assessing problems and how they would deal with them. We are now going to ask you to do the same thing in this interactive section. You will need a pen or pencil to tick items and note down your strategies for dealing with potential problems and stressors.

Before you start this exercise, you have a choice! You may prefer to read through the rest of the book first, in order to see exactly what is involved in running a business, and then come back to these pages when you have a better knowledge base from which to make your decision. Against that, you may not want to give your time to reading the book if your answers below indicate that this career move is not for you after all. We leave the choice of when to complete this exercise to you – so either get a pen or pencil, or bookmark this page!

Let's look at the checklist below. Tick the items that have encouraged you to consider setting up a coaching practice.

- Desire for independence
- Desire for additional income
- Bored or fed up with current position
- Strong dislike of current post's restrictions
- Desire for more flexible working hours
- Desire for new challenges
- Ambition
- Liking for risk-taking
- Upset caused by conflicts with other personnel in current post
- Lack of facilities in current post
- Feeling oppressed by the current regime or system
- Fed up with the office politics of the current job
- Preference for own company
- Desire a sense of achievement
- Now fully qualified and running a coaching practice is a career progression
- Desire to stand on my own two feet
- Desire to work from home, for example due to family commitments
- Other reasons: _____

  _____

  _____

  _____

These are just a few of the reasons people give us for setting up their own coaching practice. You may have included additional reasons too. Before we progress any further, return to the checklist and reflect on the items you have ticked. Then ask yourself the following questions:

- Is this a good enough reason to go into private practice?
- If I shared these reasons with my colleagues and friends, would they agree with them?

Overall, is the balance of answers you are giving yourself balanced in favour of starting your own business? If you are unsure, come back to these pages later, when you have worked systematically through this book and have a clearer idea of what is involved.

Another good exercise is to note down the pros and cons of setting up a private practice. A simple form can help you decide whether or not to take the plunge. Note how often the pros can also have cons! You will get the idea from the example Making Choices form we show you (Form 1.1), and you can then complete the blank Making Choices form (Form 1.2). You may wish to enlarge this form on a photocopier, draw the form on A4 paper or produce a similar form on your PC. This evaluation of the advantages and disadvantages is personal to you, although it may share features with our example. If there are cons, attempt to take control by noting down how you might deal with them.

Form 1.1 Making Choices Form

State problem or issue: *Starting my own coaching practice.*

Pros	Cons
Total independence from any organisation.	*This could be scary!! However, this is my second career change, and I survived the last one perfectly well.*
I can work from home at the time I choose to.	*I may see some face-to-face clients when my partner is out at work. This could be a risk. Need to consider this issue.*
I'll be able to see my children more easily.	*Working from home may mean that it will intrude into my personal life. At the moment, I leave work at the office.*
After about one year of private practice I may earn more than I do now.	*Financially it could be "touch and go" for the first six months. However, I do have some savings I could fall back on if necessary.*
I'll avoid all the petty arguments at work.	*I could have learnt how to ignore them. At least it was a good distraction.*
I need a change as I'm becoming bored. I'll start looking forward to work again.	*Work may be a bit boring, but at least I know what I'm doing. I always have my colleagues for support. I'll need to find other ways of achieving this in my own business.*
I can choose how many clients I can see in a day.	*I will need to learn more self-discipline. No more taking time off work for colds as I won't earn enough!*
I will have more control over my financial position.	*I'll be responsible for my accounts. However, I can always be guided by my accountant.*
	I don't have to balance the books at my present job. Someone else does that.

Form 1.2 **Making Choices Form**

State problem or issue:

Pros	Cons

2

Are you personally suited to being a coach?

This is the next question that you must honestly answer. Have any of the exercises helped to give you further clarity?

There are two questions that you should consider asking yourself: How determined are you? And what stresses are you likely to face?

How determined are you?

Many people start out with high expectations in the field of coaching – spending thousands of pounds on expensive coach training and envisaging that they will make a great deal of money doing something they really enjoy. The cold reality of the pressures of hard work, low income, little support, difficulty in finding clients and working on your own can be an unexpected disappointment. You may feel tired just thinking about this occurring! Be assured, you will need a great deal of determination and stamina to see you through. Stamina is a quality that is behavioural, physical and psychological. Of course, when setting up a coaching practice, everything may go well. Successful action increases confidence and leads to motivation, which stimulates the mind and energises the body. However, when having to work hard but not necessarily achieving high income or positive feedback from non-existent colleagues and very few clients, stamina may be hard to muster. The implication here is that underpinning stamina is a determined attitude of mind that focuses on the goal and does not become distracted by occasional adversity or problems.

In fact this is good news, as it means that most people can improve their stamina and motivation if they focus on modifying what they are telling themselves. You can use your own coaching skills to adjust your thinking.

What stresses are you likely to face?

Working for yourself can relieve you from certain work stresses – office politics, nine-to-five tedium and an unattractive environment, to name just a few. However, different stresses can take their place, and you need to be aware of these and know how to address them. Here are some examples of particular stresses that might come your way:

- Economic stress – for example, irregular income while becoming established, cash flow problems and no income during holiday breaks
- Physical stress – especially in later years
- Environmental stress if working from home – for example, noise, unexpected visitors, no receptionist, possibly no dedicated coaching room
- Environmental stress if renting shared office space – for example, facilities used by others, external noise, unsuitable furniture and decoration
- Competition from other practitioners
- Unsociable hours – for example, evening work
- Working in isolation
- No cover when ill
- Extensive travelling if working as an executive coach for national organisations
- Lack of administrative support
- Having to act as a cashier and take fees from clients

Which of these potential stressors have you already considered? Can you think of any more that would be specific to your own business views and ideas? Jot them down if you can. Then reflect for a few minutes on how you might attempt to deal with them and note down your answers below:

_____

_____

_____

_____

_____

_____

_____

_____

How many – if any – of these possible stressors had easy answers? If the majority did not, you may find it helpful to discuss them with an experienced colleague, or research them yourself via reading, talking with a business adviser or even running through them with a friend. You need to be prepared to deal with these (or similar) stresses. However, just in case you are not convinced these potential stressors are worth dealing with, let's consider a few of them.

Economic worries

Economic worries and concerns can become debilitating if a coach allows them to become an overwhelming issue. Although a good business plan helps, very often it is the idea that we might fail – negative "fortune telling" – that causes the real problem: "It's going to turn out badly. I'll never have enough clients to survive." You will already no doubt know quite a bit about thinking errors, yet it is amazing how often we can continue to make them ourselves. These thinking errors may trigger anxiety before an event has even happened. We will return to such errors and how to deal with them later, as they are responsible for a great deal of unnecessary stress.

Workplace issues

If you are intending to include face-to-face work with clients (as opposed to purely telephone coaching), and hire a room for a set time and day, it is likely that you will have a receptionist and possibly some administrative support. You may also have a steady stream of clients. The downside can be that you may not have been directly responsible for the furniture, room layout and so on. This can be tiresome, especially if you share the room with other business people who re-arrange the room whenever they use it. Although you may need to compromise on certain issues, such as sound-proofing the room, as a coach you will not wish to accept reduced standards. It is therefore possible that to keep overheads down (and for convenience) you may decide to set up your practice at home – which leads to its own inherent problems. While you will have considered these issues in your business plan you may not necessarily have assessed the impact upon you directly. It can be even more difficult if you live with children. Whether you are undertaking face-to-face work, or speaking with clients on the telephone, you will need a quiet atmosphere. Therefore it is important to consider very carefully the pros and cons of working from home. In addition, there is always the risk to personal security to be considered if practising from home alone. Low though the risk is, it can never be dismissed when working in an isolated environment. Of course, personal safety can be an issue in all locations and we will return to this topic again later in the book. A personal safety risk assessment should be undertaken on a regular basis.

Burnout and "rustout"

Are you working at your optimum or experiencing burnout or "rustout"? It has been suggested that as we age we may find tasks more tiring. Although our metabolic rates may gradually slow down, often feeling tired may be more a state of mind rather than a problem of age. Pacing ourselves at any age is an important part of stress management. However, in a busy coaching practice, some coaches may attempt to fit in many clients without leaving sufficient breaks between sessions, or neglect to take adequate lunch breaks. This can be compounded by working long and unsociable hours: coaching clients often want to see you during their own leisure time, rather than during the normal working day. On an occasional basis, working long hours may be acceptable, but on a regular basis it may lead to burnout. Coaches will have a wide variety of demands placed on them by their clients. Coaching clients often come (initially at least) with the idea that you are going to have all the answers to their questions. Dealing with such assumptions, and working in a very focussed and attentive way with clients, can be very stressful. At the other end of the spectrum, coaches who feel under-challenged may become bored and eventually experience rustout. If you recognise any of these issues, you may wish to consider what you can do about them, such as varying your workload or the type of client problems you deal with.

Figure 2.1 explains how rustout and burnout can develop, and what stresses you need to deal with to prevent this. Where do you appear on the diagram? On a day-to-day basis are you working at your optimum, being effective and creative, or are you fatigued or apathetic? Hopefully, you will at least be near the optimum, but if not, you are now learning the skills to do something about this.

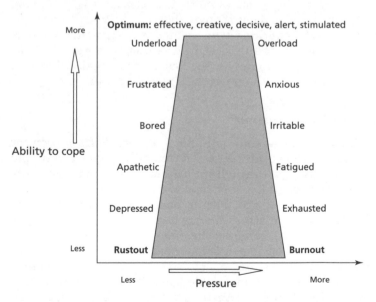

Figure 2.1 **Adapted from Palmer & Strickland (1996)**

Reflection issues

- Why do you want to enter private practice?
- What stresses might you personally face?
- How might you avoid either rustout or burnout?

Having read this section, what issues in it do you believe that you need to address?

How will you do this?

Issue	Action	By when?	Done?

By tackling these issues, what results have you achieved?

If you have been unable to tackle any of the issues you have listed, what has prevented you?

What do you need to do to rectify the situation?

3

Dealing with self-employment

Balancing your energy, expectations and workload

One of the hardest aspects of working for yourself is balancing your own input to your business. Your initial expectations as to how the business will operate may quickly be "shot down" and you will have to re-adjust your ideals to cope with reality. This in turn may mean diverting your energy into different areas.

Your workload may not be at all as you have anticipated. The belief that if you start a coaching practice, and then tell friends and family about it, clients will start to walk through the door, may soon dissipate. Individuals and companies who had assured you they would use your services seem to have changed their minds. The advertisement you ran has attracted no customers. Suddenly, although you are a coach, your job has become one of marketing, PR and administration: not uninteresting work, but very stressful when you are not bringing in any income by working on these tasks.

How can you resolve these issues, and get the balance right without exhausting yourself in the wrong areas? A good way to go about this is to divide your workload into four very distinct parts, and then to plan ahead to ensure that all of them are adequately covered. Fairley and Stout (2004) suggest that these parts, or "functions", are:

- Entrepreneurship and managerial functions – these ensure that your business is following your strategic plan, that smaller projects within the plan are up to speed, and that regular management tasks are all on schedule.

- Administrative and operations functions – these are the day-to-day functions that we have referred to in other parts of the book (for which you will wish you had a secretary!): answering the phone, paying bills, writing notes and reports, responding to queries and so on. Tedious but vital.
- Sales and marketing functions – you will know what these are in principle (if not, be sure to read our chapter on marketing) but you may not appreciate how much time you need to set aside for them.
- Technical or service functions – this is what you thought it was all about, the actual coaching work itself: your fee earner.

However good a coach you are, you will need to balance these four areas in order to run a successful business. Please do not underestimate their importance. Much as you may want simply to be a coach, it will probably take a couple of years of working hard in the other areas – especially marketing – before you can feel that you are achieving this goal.

Dealing with isolation

The majority of people are quite unaware of the way they may feel when working totally on their own. We hear about people who live alone talking of their loneliness, and possibly we sometimes feel like responding, "You should get out more!" In a working environment this is intensified, as you simply cannot "get out more". You are bound to your place of work by exactly that – it is your place of work, and in order to earn a living you need to stay in it.

If you have been used to working in a busy office, you may actually be quite shocked by how lonely you feel, and how much you miss the camaraderie, even of those work colleagues who seemed to drive you crazy when you spent every day with them. No more, "Anyone fancy a drink after work?" No more purchasing cakes for everyone when it's your birthday. No more debates about the state of the world, or the latest TV series. However, do remember that there is a difference between being alone and being lonely, and you can develop many strategies to combat what may be a new and unusual style of working.

While you may – rightly – consider coaching to be a people-orientated profession, working with clients will mean totally focussing on their needs, and will not resolve your isolation from friendly chat or professional debate – both of which are necessary for your well-being. Here are some suggestions for resolving this difficulty:

- Consider starting (or joining) a group in your area for free-lancers. These people may be running businesses quite different to yours, but there will be similar joys and difficulties that it might be helpful to talk through.
- Are there any other coaches in your area? Or would you be prepared to travel a little to meet them? If so, suggest that you get together from time to time to discuss problems and offer peer supervision for any difficult client situations.
- Look around for associations that are already established that might welcome you. Your local Chamber of Commerce or other trade associations may offer get-togethers for people running small businesses.
- Develop a network of self-employed friends you can call on from time to time, meet for lunch and so on.
- Do not spend so much time developing your business that you retreat from friendships already established. Even if your working lifestyle is now totally different to those of your friends, you will have a lot to chat about with them, and will appreciate their support.

A further problem with working alone is actually avoiding, rather than welcoming, interruptions. Unless you have rented accommodation which offers secretarial assistance or reception screening, these roles will fall to you. Obviously, when you are working with clients, either face-to-face or on the phone, you will simply not be available. However, a good proportion of your working day may see you at your desk with phones ringing, doorbells going, other family members popping their heads round the door to see if you need anything: you can picture the scenario.

With regard to phone calls, there are two obvious "assistants". The first is caller ID: you will not miss the urgent client call you are waiting for, but will not find yourself on the other end of the line to Auntie Joan, who wants to tell you about her hernia operation (a dedicated business telephone line will also help you out of this sort of difficulty). The second is a message service. If you are especially disciplined, you can change the message regularly to reflect your availability/non-availability during the day. If you do this, clients will not expect a return call until the time you've indicated you will be free.

It is also possible to sign up to a professional telephone answering service. For a monthly fee, your calls will be diverted to a permanently manned answering service, where your business name "J. Bloggs and Associates" is used on answering the call, and a message taken, just as though you have a personal receptionist. Messages are then relayed to you promptly and accurately. This might be well worth considering as your business builds up.

If you have great difficulty not answering a ringing phone, then turn the ringtone off when you do not wish to be interrupted. Messages will still come through, but you will not be disturbed (or curious!).

When working from home, family interruptions can be tempered by a sign on the door when you're busy. In an office away from home, you may be able to ask a receptionist to screen calls or make sure no-one interrupts you.

If you are totally alone in your home or office, it seems almost like a reflex action to answer the doorbell when it rings. Don't! Unless you are expecting someone, the chances are it will not be urgent, and may be a time-wasting enquiry about double glazing, re-surfacing your drive or some such thing.

The other side of being alone is that you may become a little reclusive: you may actually enjoy the isolation a little too much! Ensure you do not let this happen at the expense of losing touch with what is going on in your profession in the wider world, or with the communications you need to maintain in order to keep your marketing campaign moving onwards and upwards.

Balancing your working day, with the right amount and the right sort of communication with others, may not come easily to you, but it is essential to your well-being. Spend time on the planning and self-discipline you will need to ensure that you have got this right.

Keeping yourself creative

We discussed burnout and rustout in an earlier section. We have also discussed the different areas of the business that need attention in order to create and maintain a viable whole. However, it is also very important to know how to keep yourself in a positive, creative mind-set.

As a coach, you may well be helping other people to achieve this on a regular basis. But in the same way that many accountants we know leave their own financial affairs in a hopeless mess, and hairdressers who create wonderful styles for others walk around looking as though their own hair has never seen a brush, it may be quite possible for you to omit to look at your own thoughts about the business and your abilities to make it successful. For this reason, we would like to spend some time looking at the thinking errors that can lead to negative speculation and assumptions. These errors are especially likely to occur when we are tired or stressed, when clients have cancelled or unexpected bills have come in, and we are beginning to wonder if the whole idea is a mistake.

To counteract this, we need to look at the thinking errors we might be making, in order to modify our perceptions and beliefs. This will help to tackle procrastination, lack of motivation, stress and reduced performance, thus encouraging more creativity and higher performance levels.

Challenging thinking errors with thinking skills

When we become stressed we usually have a variety of negative or unconstructive thoughts, which in turn prevent us from being able to resolve the problem effectively. Psychologists have identified 14 common thinking errors. By identifying and challenging these thinking errors, our stress levels can be reduced.

As you read about the thinking errors below, ask yourself whether you have ever had these or similar thoughts – and whether one or more of these errors has ever prevented you from successfully resolving a problem. After each stress-inducing thinking error we suggest a constructive, stress-reducing thinking skill you can use that may help to counter or challenge the error.

Let's now take a look at the specific thinking errors.

Error: labelling

You negatively globally label yourself or others instead of rating specific skills or behaviours. For example: "Because I have not achieved my coaching accreditation, I am a complete failure," or, "My accountant has made a mistake. This proves she is a total idiot and incompetent."

Skill: de-labelling

Do you find labelling helpful in dealing with situations? Is this style of thinking motivating or de-motivating? Does it decrease or increase your anger? What happens to your stress levels? Does it make you feel happy?

Step back and ask yourself how realistic and valid these global labels are. Are they an accurate description? Most people discover it is less stressful to rate specific aspects/deficits instead of using a global rating. Constructive alternatives could be: "Failing to achieve my accreditation does not mean that I'm a complete failure as a human being," or, "When my accountant makes a mistake, all it proves is that she is a fallible person like the rest of us."

Error: all-or-nothing thinking

This involves viewing situations or problems only in extreme terms with no middle ground. For example: "If I'm going to rent offices then I'll go for the best," or, "So many things are going wrong at work I may as well go into business on my own."

Skill: relative thinking

Attempt to find the middle ground, or look for shades of grey. Constructive alternatives could be: "I don't have to go for the best, which is probably too expensive, in the first year of private practice. Good enough will do," or, "Things may be going wrong at work but many things happen that are great or just OK as well. Perhaps I should look at the overall picture and maintain a realistic perspective."

Error: focussing on the negative

You focus on the negative aspects of a situation or event, while ignoring the positive. For example: when running a workshop, only dwelling on a few negative student feedback evaluation forms ("The course was boring") rather than focusing on the overall comments, or ignoring positive feedback given by your colleagues – "They may think I've done a good job, but I made so many mistakes I really messed up that project."

Skill: focussing on the overall picture

Instead of just focussing on the negative, attempt to focus on the overall picture, including the positive. Constructive alternatives could be: "Certain parts of the course were boring but there were good parts too," or, "In fact I made only five mistakes and we reached the agreed targets."

Error: discounting the positive

You consider all positive events as unimportant and disregard them. For example: "My client only came back because his company was paying," rather than acknowledging that you used your coaching skills well, or, "My associate has only referred clients on to me that she doesn't want herself."

Skill: counting the positive

When people do well or receive good feedback from others, they can choose to accept the positive results. Constructive alternatives could be: "The client came back because he found the coaching productive and helpful," or, "My associate has passed clients on to me because she knows I am a good coach."

Error: magnification or "awfulising"

You exaggerate the significance of an event or problem out of all proportion. With stress, this involves focussing on the negative, sometimes known as "awfulising". For example: "If I don't make sufficient profit in my coaching practice it will be the end of the world," or, "It's absolutely awful not to have a wider variety of clients."

Skill: demagnification or "de-awfulising"

In most situations the outcome is seldom really awful or the end of the world, but our thinking makes it so. By making a mountain out of a molehill we lose perspective. This is responsible for much unnecessary stress. Questions to counter this thinking include: What aspect of this situation is bad? Will it really be that important in three, six or twelve months from now? Is it really the end of the world? Am I losing sight of the overall picture?

Constructive alternatives could be: "If I don't make sufficient profit in my practice I could always get paid employment again. This would be a pain but not the end of the world," or, "Not having a wide variety of clients is limiting, but not dreadful. As my business builds up, this will probably change."

Error: minimisation

This is the opposite of magnification. It involves playing down the importance of our achievements, strengths and skills. For example: "Becoming a qualified coach was nothing," or, "When I've done well, it's always down to luck."

Skill: taking personal responsibility

Consider what you are responsible for in a particular situation. Avoid downplaying your involvement. Take responsibility for your actions, whether positive or negative. Constructive alternatives could be: "I actually worked really hard to achieve my coaching qualifications," or, "On reflection, my good luck is in direct proportion to my hard work."

Error: mind-reading

You make assumptions that people are either thinking or reacting negatively towards you based on the absence of evidence to the contrary. For example: "The company hasn't yet returned my call. Perhaps they don't think I am a good coach," or, "My girlfriend is unhappy with all the time I am giving to my business. She hasn't asked me about it for weeks."

Skill: considering possible alternatives

Stressed people have a tendency to interpret others' actions or behaviours in a negative manner. This is often based on little evidence. Challenge your mind-reading. Consider the alternatives. Ask yourself: Are there any other possible reasons for the person's behaviour? Am I making a negative interpretation when I could make a positive interpretation? Constructive alternatives could be: "Perhaps the company is focussing on its merger with another firm," or, "Perhaps my girlfriend is preoccupied with her own work problems, or simply believes that my business is going well."

Error: fortune-telling

You predict a negative outcome for events despite the fact there is a lack of evidence to support your prediction. For example: "I'm bound to get into debt starting my own business," or, "The presentation will almost certainly go wrong."

Skill: reality check

How realistic are your powers of negative clairvoyance? Rate your predicted outcome of the particular event on a scale of 0 to 100, where 0 is "certain not to happen" and 100 is "certain to happen". Constructive alternatives could be: "If I carefully manage my business I am unlikely to get into debt," or, "I may make a few mistakes but it is unlikely that the whole presentation will go totally pear-shaped."

Errors: personalisation and blame

You blame yourself for outcomes for which you are not entirely responsible. For example: "My client did not make the progress we had hoped for, in spite of my best efforts," or, "The group work got cancelled and it's all my fault."

Blame is the opposite of personalisation. This is where you blame others, ignoring any effect your own attitudes or behaviours may have on the outcome. For example: "My clients do not improve as they are never willing to work hard," or, "Nobody told me that I had to pay VAT bills on time."

Skill: broadening the picture

Constructive alternatives to personalisation could be: "I'm being unrealistic. I can't assume that all my clients will make progress regardless of my own good skills," or, "There are a wide variety of reasons that the work got cancelled that will have nothing to do with me."

Constructive alternatives to blame could be" "My clients may not improve as quickly as I would like, but they do try their best," or, "I am responsible for finding out about VAT payments. In future I will carefully read the VAT forms."

A useful technique for challenging personalisation or blame is to note down all the individuals or issues involved and then represent these different people and issues graphically on a pie chart. This will allow you to allocate everybody's responsibility for what happened, including your own. See Figures 3.1 and 3.2 for examples of this technique.

Error: emotional reasoning

You evaluate a situation based purely on how you feel emotionally. For example: "Getting that wrong makes me feel like a complete idiot – so I must be one," or, "I feel so anxious. Giving this presentation will obviously be impossible."

Skill: keeping emotions in their place

Remind yourself that just because you are feeling an intense negative emotion, it does not necessarily mean that you are in a stressful or anger- or anxiety-provoking situation. Check with others how they might respond to such a situation, to get a better idea of how accurate your own views are and whether such an emotional response would be likely for them as well. Often people misunderstand a situation or mishear what was said,

Case study 1

Situation: Sarah was asked to work with a team of people within a company, to increase their motivation to reach a specific work target. When this did not happen, she felt totally responsible for the situation (personalisation; see top pie chart). Sarah then used the "broaden the picture" technique and realised she was not completely responsible (see bottom pie chart) and there were other factors that had contributed to the team not meeting their target.

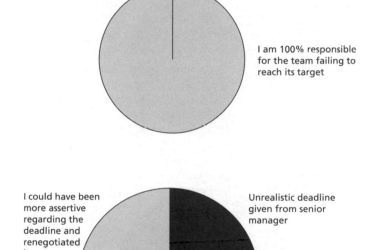

Figure 3.1   **From Palmer et al. (2003)**

Case study 2

Situation: Peter had quite a heavy client caseload at exactly the same time that he was negotiating for some new premises. He asked his partner, Fay, if she could deal with this for him, which she willingly agreed to do, although she was a little concerned about some of the complexities of the transaction. In the event, she made a mistake in her understanding of what negotiating was required, and the deal fell through. Peter blamed Fay totally for the loss of his new office space.

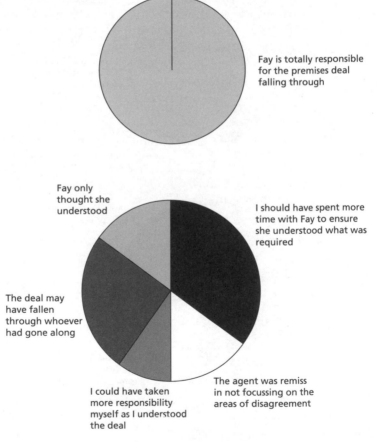

Fay is totally responsible for the premises deal falling through

Fay only thought she understood

I should have spent more time with Fay to ensure she understood what was required

The deal may have fallen through whoever had gone along

I could have taken more responsibility myself as I understood the deal

The agent was remiss in not focussing on the areas of disagreement

Figure 3.2 **From Palmer et al. (2003)**

misconstrue what was meant or do not have the facts. Constructive alternatives could be: "Making mistakes does not mean I'm a complete idiot," or, "Although I may feel anxious, people give presentations all the time, and I have also presented well before, so it is obviously not impossible."

Error: over-generalisation

This involves taking one unfortunate event and then drawing sweeping, generalised conclusions about all other events, usually with insufficient evidence. For example: "Client A cancelled. I expect this is the start of everyone cancelling," or, "Because I didn't get that contract, I'm unlikely to be offered any other work."

Skill: focus on the information available

Avoid drawing inferences or conclusions based on little evidence. Wait until you have more evidence available before you draw negative conclusions. Constructive alternatives could be: "My client cancelled for a specific reason. This won't affect anyone else," or, "Not getting that particular contract does not mean that there won't be other opportunities. I need to be persistent and increase my marketing."

Error: "demanding-ness"

This occurs when you hold fixed, rigid and absolute beliefs, which often result in unrealistic expectations of yourself and others. These are usually expressed as "musts", "shoulds", "got tos", "have tos" and "oughts". For example: "I must always arrive on time," or, "Mistakes must not be made."

Skill: thinking coolly and flexibly

Challenge your demanding language. For example: Where is it written that I must? Who said I should? Is this flexible thinking? Then introduce flexible, non-demanding, non-absolute beliefs that consist of preferential wishes and desires. Constructive alternatives could be: "Although it is strongly preferable to

Form 3.1   **Exercise: thinking errors audit**

We advocate undertaking a personal audit of thinking errors. Think about a past, current or future issue you are frustrated or stressed about. Write down your stress-inducing thoughts associated with the issue or problem. Next, note the thinking errors you recognise in yourself.

Stress-inducing thoughts (SITs)

_____

_____

Thinking errors	Your example
Labelling	
All-or-nothing thinking	
Focussing on the negative	
Discounting the positive	
Magnification	
Minimisation	
Mind-reading	
Fortune-telling	
Personalisation	
Blame	
Emotional reasoning	
Over-generalisation	
"Demanding-ness"	
"I-can't-stand-it-itis"	

Additional thinking skills

A number of additional thinking skills may help you to reduce stress and increase creative performance.

- Befriend yourself: befriending is a powerful thinking skill many of us already possess but seldom use on ourselves to counter unhelpful, self-critical thoughts. When a colleague or friend makes an error, what supportive statements would you generally make? It is likely that you would not be critical or harsh, but instead positively encouraging. However, notice that you may be harsh on yourself in the same circumstances. Instead of thinking, "I was useless at giving the presentation," stand back and think about it more realistically. "Actually, in the whole hour I only made two or three errors. That's not bad considering it was my second presentation." By accepting that you made errors, and by being supportive when you focus on the positive aspects, your internal dialogue will reduce stress and maintain motivation.
- Look for evidence: challenge your stress-inducing ideas by looking for evidence, instead of making assumptions. Ask others for feedback about a task you have undertaken, such as chairing a meeting or making a presentation. You can also test assumptions by deploying behavioural interventions. For example, if you believe that you can't stand waiting in supermarket queues, make yourself select the longest queue to wait in next time you shop, and practise distraction – perhaps start a conversation with the person standing in front of or behind you. This will provide you with proof that you are able to stand the waiting, even if you do not particularly like it. It is important to avoid mind-reading.

Questions to challenge your stress-inducing thinking and thinking errors

The use of challenging questions is an excellent method to help you examine the validity of your stress-inducing thinking and your thinking errors. Think back to the earlier exercise when you noted down your thinking errors. Write down below your stress-inducing statement and thinking error. Then choose questions from the examples below that would help you to challenge its validity (Palmer & Strickland, 1996):

Statement: _____

Thinking error: _____

_____

Is the belief logical?

- Would a scientist agree with it?
- Where is the belief written, apart from in my own head?
- Am I labelling myself, or somebody or something else? Is this a logical thing to do?

Is the belief realistic (empirically correct)?

- Where is the evidence for my belief?
- Would people I know agree with my idea? Is the situation so awful or terrible? What is making it feel this way?
- Am I making a big deal of this? Am I blowing it out of proportion?
- If I "can't stand it", what will really happen?

Is the belief helpful/pragmatic?

- Where is my attitude getting me?
- Is it helping me attain my goals?
- Is my belief helping me to solve my problem?
- Am I placing demands on others or myself? Is this helpful and constructive?
- Am I taking things too personally?

The questions listed below are designed to enable you to move forward and develop more effective beliefs (adapted Palmer & Whybrow, 2004):

- What are the consequences for my goals if I hold on to this belief?
- Are there any advantages for me in holding on to this belief?

- What is the evidence for and against this belief?
- Would I ask my family and friends to share this belief?
- What experiments could I conduct to test the truth or falsity of this belief?
- In what way does this belief make sense to me?
- What suggestions would I make to a friend with a belief similar to mine?
- Do I still want to be stuck with this block in one/three/six months' time?
- Is this belief rigid or flexible?
- If I was giving advice to myself as an impartial observer, what suggestions would I offer to deal with this block?
- If I was presenting my belief to a jury of my peers, is it likely they would be persuaded by my arguments?
- How would I sum up the case for and against my belief?
- What would be a more helpful belief to adopt in order to overcome this block?
- How can I prove to myself that this belief is more helpful?

In the next section, when using the worksheets, these questions can be applied to help you to challenge your stress-inducing thoughts and performance-interfering thinking.

Stress thought record

Stress thought records involve noting down the thinking errors or the stress-inducing thoughts you are experiencing. These can be referred to as stress-inducing thinking (SIT). Once you have identified which thoughts are exacerbating your stress you can begin to apply the thinking skills discussed previously, and develop thoughts to alleviate the stress, known as stress-alleviating thinking (SAT; developed by Neenan and Palmer, at the Centre for Stress Management).

Exercise

There follows an example of a stress thought record (Form 3.2), then a blank stress thought record form (Form 3.3). Complete the blank form for a problem you wish to feel less stressed about, or a fear you have about setting up your business. Note down in

Form 3.2 **Stress thought record**

Stress inducing thinking (SIT)	Stress alleviating thinking (SAT)
If my coaching practice fails it will impact upon my family and finances.	*Worrying won't decrease the likelihood of failure – it will probably make it worse if anything. I have lots of skills if this does go wrong. I shouldn't have too much of a problem finding other work.*
I am not sure if I can handle taking such a risk.	*Of course I can. I am a competent and experienced coach and have done a great deal of research on running my own business.*
I am worried that I will not generate enough clients to earn a reasonable income.	*I have gone into my financial situation in great detail, and have made provision for not earning a great deal while I am building the business up. I will be fine financially.*
I'm concerned that my life now will be "all work and no play". The possibility of burnout really worries me.	*Starting my own business is something that I have always wanted to do. I am far more likely to regret not taking this opportunity.*
	I will take steps to balance my work/non-work life, and enlist the help of friends and family to ensure that I stick to this.
	I will find time for some exercise each week, and make sure that I eat well for fitness. This will give me more energy.
	I can keep reviewing the situation. If things really do pile up, I can always find an associate to work with me: money isn't everything.

© Centre for Stress Management, 2001

Form 3.3 **Stress thought record**

Stress inducing thinking (SIT)	Stress alleviating thinking (SAT)

the SIT column any of your thoughts, attitudes or thinking errors that increase stress. Then use the questions and thinking skills from the previous sections to challenge your SIT and help you to develop SAT, and complete the SAT column.

Improving performance under pressure

Do you want to increase your performance when under pressure? Certainly when setting up and running your business, you are likely to experience periods of high pressure and sometimes you may find that you are not achieving what you would like to. Or, conversely, when you are not under pressure you may find that you waste time and become unproductive. In both of these circumstances it is possible that you may have performance interfering thoughts (PITs). These can be noted down on an Enhancing Performance form and new performance enhancing thoughts (PETs) can be developed. This method was developed by Neenan and Palmer at the Centre for Coaching and is similar to using the stress thought record.

Exercise

There follows an example of a completed Enhancing Performance form (Form 3.4), then a blank one. Complete the blank one for a situation related to your work in which you wish to improve your performance. Note down below in the PIT column any of your thoughts, attitudes or thinking errors that interfere with or reduce your performance. Then use the thinking skills or questions from the earlier sections as an aid to challenge your PIT, and develop and note down in the PET column your new performance enhancing thoughts.

Using imagery techniques for coping and motivation

A range of imagery techniques can help us either to prepare for potentially stressful or difficult situations or to motivate us (Palmer & Dryden, 1995). In this section we cover two important techniques, coping and motivation imagery, both of which may help you in setting up your business.

Form 3.4 Enhancing performance form

State problem: *Giving a poor presentation*

Performance interfering thinking (PIT)	Performance enhancing thinking (PET)
I "must" perform well.	*Although it's strongly preferable to perform well, realistically I don't have to.*
Otherwise the outcome will be awful.	*If I don't perform well, the outcome will be bad but hardly awful and devastating. Certainly not the end of the world!!!*
I'll never get that contract.	*"All or nothing" thinking and "fortune telling" again! It's unlikely I'll be judged on one event.*
This will prove I'm totally useless.	*It may prove I have presentation skills deficits but not that I'm useless. Perhaps instead of avoiding presentations, in future I need to get more practice by offering to do them!*

© Centre for Coaching, 2003

Form 3.5 Enhancing performance form

State problem:

Performance interfering thinking (PIT)	Performance enhancing thinking (PET)

Coping imagery

Coping imagery involves picturing yourself coping with the situation you are feeling stressed about and challenging the negative imagery that is winding you up. It is important to note this is called "coping imagery" and not "mastery imagery", whereby you imagine yourself completing the task perfectly (McMullin, 1986). Many people who are feeling stressed about a future feared event do not have the confidence to believe they will ever be able to master the situation. However, they are able to imagine themselves coping because this allows for the realistic element of fallibility (Palmer et al., 2003).

For example, accepting that you will be able to present a perfect conference paper is unlikely, but giving a paper that is good enough is more realistic. Coping imagery can also help to deal with phobias or difficult social situations. It can be useful to prevent negative images raising stress levels, which may later become self-fulfilling prophecies if not tackled.

Coping imagery exercise

There are five steps in this exercise:

- Think of a future event you are feeling anxious or stressed about.
- Write down the particular aspects of this situation that you are feeling most stressed about.
- Think of ways to overcome these problems. You may want to speak with a friend or partner if you are unable to think of a way to deal with the problem yourself.
- Now visualise yourself in the situation that you fear and, using the strategies you have identified in Step 3, slowly imagine yourself coping. Picture yourself dealing with the problems as they arise. You may need to repeat this procedure three or four times.
- Practise this technique regularly, especially when you find yourself feeling stressed about a situation or event.

Motivation imagery

Motivation imagery was developed by Palmer and Neenan (1998) to help de-motivated people become more motivated and prepare themselves for action. It can be used for both personal and work-related problems. The first stage is to imagine not doing what you want to do for the rest of your life, and the second stage is to visualise actually doing what you want to do.

Motivation imagery exercise

Think about an area in your life that you could improve by taking action which until now you have avoided. This could include setting up your own business, or leaving a relationship, for example.

- Visualise yourself for the rest of your life not undertaking the change. What effect will it have on you or your friends and family? What regrets would you have if you did nothing?
- Now, imagine yourself doing what you would like to do and think about the short- and long-term benefits that the change would make to your life.
- Finally, consider how you are going to put the change into action.

It is very important to visualise the "inaction" imagery before the "action" imagery, in order to motivate yourself. Do not use this technique if you are depressed.

We hope that the skills we have discussed in this section will be extremely useful to you personally. We also hope that they will be useful to your clients as well, in helping them to pinpoint blocks that might be holding them back, and in making the necessary changes to move forward.

Reflection issues

- Which thinking errors or beliefs could hold you back from progressing with your goal of setting up a private coaching practice?

arrive on time, realistically sometimes I'll arrive late," or, "Just because I wish everything to be error-free, that does not mean that there will never be mistakes."

Error: "I-can't-stand-it-itis"

By telling yourself, "I can't stand it," or, "I can't bear it," you reduce your tolerance for dealing with frustrating or difficult problems. For example: "I can't stand my clients turning up late," or, "I can't bear doing boring paperwork." This style of thinking leads to the lowering of one's tolerance for dealing with frustration or stressful events. This is known as low frustration tolerance (LFT).

Skill: developing high frustration tolerance (HFT)

Accepting reality and challenging LFT beliefs are important. Ask yourself: Where is the evidence that I can't stand it? How long have I been standing it? The task, albeit quite hard, is to develop new beliefs that change LFT to HFT. Constructive alternatives could be: "I may not like it but I can obviously tolerate it if clients turn up late. It is their own time, in any event," or, "If I just accept that sometimes I have to do boring paperwork – as do many others – then I will be less frustrated and will complete it more quickly."

Thinking errors audit

Before we go any further and include other thinking skills, it might be an idea now to stop and take stock of the thinking errors you may make on a daily basis, or when you are in stressful situations. The exercise in Form 3.1 will help you to focus on your thinking errors (Cooper & Palmer, 2000).

By identifying your thinking errors when you are stressed or under-performing, you will be in a better position to appraise the problem or assess the pressures more realistically. This process of thinking about your thinking will help to distance you from your stress-inducing thoughts and the negative feelings that arise from them. Thus, even though this is an audit, it may help you to reduce stress and increase performance.

- Do you have any goal-blocking PITs? How could you tackle them?
- Would your clients find thinking skills useful?

Having read this section, what issues in it do you believe that you need to address?

How will you do this?

Issue	Action	By when?	Done?

By tackling these issues, what results have you achieved?

If you have been unable to tackle any of the issues you have listed, what has prevented you?

What do you need to do to rectify the situation?

PART 2

Making your business work

4

Causes of success vs. failure

Minimising the risks

One of the reactions of friends and colleagues when you announce your intention to start your own business can be: "Isn't that a bit risky?" There is of course a lot of truth in this comment, but in this day and age there is very little employment that is secure for life. On the plus side, many self-employed people will say "At least I cannot get the sack!", which is also very true.

Of course, even paid employment frequently involves risk taking. Many people suffer from stress, working long hours in jobs where the pressures are difficult to cope with, they have little control over day-to-day events, unsatisfactory relationships with bosses or colleagues and little sense of achievement. Families, a social life and personal health can be ignored until it is too late.

In a private coaching practice some of these concerns are relieved, but replaced by others. You need to give realistic consideration to the following points:

- Your time may be your own but you must use it to create and meet a demand for your services. As a rule of thumb, you will need to spend about 40% of your time developing your business – and you will not be earning an income for this portion of your time.
- You will not have an employer who will provide paid work, paid holidays, paid sick or maternity leave, working premises, equipment, materials, pension schemes, training etc. It is extraordinary how even the use of office pens, coffee makers,

telephone calls, stationery pads etc. can be taken for granted until we have to start supplying all these things for ourselves.

- You may work largely in isolation, without the support of colleagues. This is not necessarily a bad thing as many employees (possibly some of your future clients) find office politics very stressful, but you will need to consider meeting your own needs for support and company.

- Worries about redundancy are replaced by worries about not generating sufficient income to survive and meet your outgoings.

- You alone have to take responsibility for building and sustaining a credible and acceptable professional reputation.

- You will have to deal with your own paperwork and keep records and accounts. Computer skills will become more important – there won't be an IT department to sort your computer out just before an important PowerPoint presentation.

- It will be important to keep a balance between your personal life, meeting the needs of clients, maintaining high standards and making a reasonable living. Without the structure of a nine-to-five working day, you will need to consider the needs of your family and commit to some type of self-disciplined schedule that will not cause undue stress to yourself or to those whose support you need for your venture.

We hope that by the time you have worked through this book, we will have provided possible solutions to the above issues, or at the very least given you some ideas for tackling them yourself in the way that is best for you personally.

We also want to stress that there is a myriad of exciting positives to working for yourself that will make the risks very worthwhile and we do not wish to discourage you from focussing on these. It is simply that our task in this section of the book is to help you avoid the pitfalls.

While it is undoubtedly true that some of the most useful lessons are learnt from taking risks and making mistakes, it is necessary to balance risk with caution. It is therefore important to be aware of risk, and to understand it as a concept, rather than simply plough forward with a "wing and a prayer" approach.

There are three basic types of risk:

- Risks you can afford to take. For example, you may be asked to give a presentation to an evening group, which might generate some new business. The only risk here would be if you gave a bad presentation.
- Risks you cannot afford to take. For example, you may be asked to do some work for a company you know is a notoriously bad payer and whose present finances are in poor shape. Even though you could use the work, the chances are you will have difficulty recovering your money, if you recover it at all, and this could seriously damage your business.
- Risks you cannot afford not to take. For example, you may set your fee scale very low in order to encourage new business. Then, in an attempt to meet your financial outgoings you may find yourself seeing more clients than you can comfortably manage and have little time for anything else. You know you should reduce the number of clients and raise your fees but fear a drop in business. However, you reduce client numbers and raise fees.

You will need to understand the principles of risk assessment (placing a risk into one of the above categories and deciding whether or not it is sensible to take) and risk management (having a plan in place that will pick up the pieces if things do go wrong).

In a sense, much of this book is concerned with turning unmanaged risks into managed risks, reducing uncertainty and enabling coaches to take more control of their chosen profession. Some risks are unavoidable but following sound business, professional and ethical principles will ensure that these are sensibly evaluated, and won't be so great as to ruin you.

Risk-taking can be scary but it can also be exciting and the challenges it presents can be invigorating. The very act of setting up in business on your own shows you to be a risk-taker, and if you marry this up with positive action and doing what it takes to make your business work, you have excellent chances of great success.

Why businesses fail

You may well be aware that a large proportion of small businesses do fail, and often this can be for reasons outside their control – changes in government policy, rules and regulations, taxes, the closure of an essential supplier or a reduced demand for their product or service due to a new innovation taking its place.

However, this is not always the case and many small businesses fail due to inexperience, lack of (essential) knowledge, lack of foresight and either not having, or not sticking to, a viable business plan. Yet in many cases such disappointments are avoidable.

Good all-round preparation will reduce unnecessary risks. Spending time now can save time later and prevent insurmountable difficulties. It does not eliminate the unexpected but it helps you to be much more prepared for dealing with it when it happens.

If you are thinking of setting up your own private practice, good preparation will undoubtedly improve your chances of success. As to what you need to prepare, this is covered in the sections that follow. Let us look now at some of the specific reasons that small businesses can fail.

The original idea was not thought through

When John decided to set up his own private coaching practice, he decided that he would offer both telephone coaching and face-to-face consultations for those who were happier to speak with their coach in person rather than down a telephone line.

He considered renting premises, but felt that he was making a wise financial decision to use his own home – a flat that had a spare room that could easily be converted into a coaching office. John decided to spend time and money making the environment both professional and relaxing so that clients would feel at ease and truly benefit from the sessions. He was very proud of the environment he created.

Eventually, John gave his notice in at work and took the plunge, using his marketing and advertising skills to create a clientele. He was exceedingly successful and very soon had a large number of enquiries for his services. He decided to offer a complimentary first coaching session hoping that at least a proportion would be followed up by on-going, paid bookings. So he was very surprised when he discovered that he failed to convert almost all of his enquiries into on-going clients after their initial visit. They simply did not come back.

John did not consider that his coaching skills were at fault as the clients had seemed most receptive during the sessions. In the end, he decided that he would contact a sample of these people and simply ask them, in a polite way, if they would be willing to let him know why they had decided against returning.

The replies caused him to kick himself for his short-sightedness. Almost everyone told him that the problem was the general environment. Although John's coaching room was excellent, he lived in a run-down area where dubious people hung around on street corners, graffiti ranged over the walls of his building, the lobby of his apartment block was dirty and unkempt and there was nowhere safe to park.

In this case, financial economy was also financial suicide, and John needed to relocate premises in order to make his business viable.

Insufficient income

The idea that making money is a "numbers game" – the more you sell the more you make – is only relevant when you have an unlimited supply of the product. Selling your time is always going to be a finite operation.

One young coach, Anne, who was very keen to build up her practice as quickly as she could, decided that the best way to do this was to offer very discounted rates for the foreseeable future, simply to build up her clientele.

This she certainly managed to do. Clients were delighted that they could book several coaching sessions with Anne for the cost of just one session with others they had contacted, and very soon she had almost more clients than she could service. However, Anne not only became exhausted from overwork but her income, following cost deductions, hardly made it worth her while working at all.

Anne realised that she would have to restructure her fee scales completely and accept that a slowly built up business was a more lucrative option in the long run.

Insufficient working capital

Katherine was determined to learn from the experiences of John and Anne to make a success of private practice. She found premises in a very pleasant location at a rent of £400 per month and signed a 12-month tenancy agreement. She saw her bank manager and managed to get an unsecured loan of £4,000 repayable over two years. She spent £3,000 of the loan on the deposit for the room, a computer, furniture and furnishings and general office items, leaving £1,000 "to be on the safe side". She decided she would be charging clients £35 per session.

Katherine had moved back to live with her parents when her relationship broke down and she reckoned she could manage on living expenses of £600 a month. Her parents were happy to support her in her business venture as they could see the long-term advantages for their daughter. What could go wrong?

Clients started arriving, paid their fees and booked repeat sessions. Katherine felt encouraged. However, although client numbers were steadily increasing they were not doing so as quickly as Katherine had imagined they would. She was surprised how quickly the spare £1,000 from her bank loan disappeared although she had been very strict with her own personal expenditure.

After three months Katherine had run out of cash and was concerned about her tenancy agreement. She reviewed her income and expenditure. Her records showed:

Income (3 months)		Expenditure (3 months)	
Month 1: 16 clients @ £35	£560	Deposit premises	£400
Month 2: 24 clients @ £35	£840	Rent	£1200
Month 3: 40 clients @ £35	£1400	Loan repayments	£600
		Telephone bills	£400
		Living expenses	£1800
Sub-total	£2800	Sub-total	£4400
Deficit financed by:			
Remaining bank loan	£1000		
Personal savings	£600		
Total	£4400	Total	£4400

Faced with a drop in income over the Christmas period, the cancellation of a skiing holiday in January, the exhaustion of her own remaining personal savings and the probable sale of her car, Katherine approached her landlord, who agreed to cancel her lease in return for retaining the initial deposit. The bank loan repayments were re-scheduled over a longer time period and Katherine arranged for colleagues to take over her clients.

Insufficient financial control

The idea that being a good coach will ensure that the financial side of things will take care of itself doesn't always work out. An excellent coach known to us paid no attention to his accounting throughout the year, although he had an excellent client list and was very successful. He tended to assume that if he took a look at his financial paperwork at tax return time that would be enough – and was horrified to discover, when that time came, that his relaxed spending habits had left him with too little to pay his tax bill. He had forgotten about his credit card spending, never noted down his personal outgoings and simply hoped that it would all work out. This was a real shame as his coaching skills were excellent. Hiring an accountant turned things around for him, but not without a great deal of early worry and heartache.

Insufficient skills

The other side of the coin is the person who thinks that anyone can be a coach.

Jane was a good businesswoman who wanted a change of direction. She had seen a corporate coach at work in her own organisation and thought that this seemed an easy way to earn a living. Jane decided that since coach training was not mandatory, she would not bother with it: she felt that she knew enough anyway to come across fairly well. Advertising her services, she drew many initial enquiries.

However, Jane had little idea of self-employment generally, was uncertain what rates to charge people or how to deal with them professionally – all skills that she might have learned had she bothered with some training. Clients rarely returned after their first session and Jane soon became very despondent that she had not taken time to increase her skills base before embarking on such a career change.

Lack of motivation and energy

We have briefly referred already to the importance of good preparation, and lack of this can run a coaching practice into the ground very quickly.

Peter was a charming man and initially clients warmed to him and felt they were in the hands of a good coach. However, his easy-going attitude to life spilled over into his practice. Clients would telephone at a pre-arranged time and discover that Peter was not there (or at least, not answering his telephone). He was often late for face-to-face meetings and when going into corporate settings would find that his clients had had to move on to further business meetings. When he saw clients at home, he often could not find the relevant files and wasted precious time on this.

Peter did not come across as motivated or energetic with his laissez-faire attitude and quickly went out of business: clients gave up on him, with no desire to give him a second chance despite his ever-charming apologies.

Hardworking and conscientious to the point of breakdown

The issue of professional boundaries can be a very difficult one when working independently in a client-service profession. What do you do when clients call between sessions for further advice or disturb evenings and weekends? Or when you find it hard to say no to new business, even though you can scarcely fit in the clients you already have?

Nicholas fell into this category but failed to see what his problem was until it was too late. He was actually flattered that his clients seemed to depend on him so much and thrilled that his business was taking off so well. He tried very hard to accommodate clients' appointment time wishes and always agreed to evening and weekend work if that suited them better.

In the end, he was working almost a seven-day week, with much of it unpaid as clients made extra calls and discovered that Nicholas would invariably speak to them, rather than direct them to their next pre-booked appointment time.

It was little wonder that Nicholas eventually suffered from burnout as the stress of it all overtook him and his practice collapsed.

Family pressures

Many people see one of the joys of freelancing as having more time with the family. They feel that they can juggle their working hours to fit around children's needs and be at home at times they would otherwise be in an office.

Reality can be quite different. One female coach we know decided that continuing this career from home when she had her first child would be ideal. Susan would work while the baby napped and be free to play with the baby when he was awake. She also saw coaching as a profession that would be suited to evening work when the baby was asleep. The only problem was that the baby didn't sleep in the day, and often did not sleep continuously at night either. Susan quickly realised that without better organisation and outside help, her business would not survive.

David also decided to create a home office for his coaching business. As his children grew he valued the idea of being there when they came home from school and simply being close by, even though he planned to set up an office environment for his work. In reality, when clients called it was often impossible to keep the children quiet and the sound of their noise in the background made David look distinctly unprofessional. As well as this, David's wife would often interrupt him to do errands for her or to child-sit as the temptation of knowing he was in the house proved too great. David soon learned that he needed to relocate to rented office space to keep his practice going.

The wrong location

Philip's corporate coaching business was going exceedingly well in the city in which he lived but he and his family longed to move to a more rural location. They found a country home that they loved, taking into account the travelling time that Philip would need to continue to work with the same clients. At first, everything seemed idyllic, but this changed when two of Philip's major clients relocated and the journey time from the country area in which he now lived became impossible. Philip tried to replace this lost business in the locality of his home, but there simply was not the demand for this type of work outside of the major city corporations he had been working with. He tried to increase his personal coaching work but, again, the demand simply was not there. In the end, Philip had to rent a flat during the week to remain near to his core business while the family considered their future living arrangements.

Unforeseen circumstances

While bad luck is obviously outside our control, we do need to be aware that it can fall our way – and perhaps needs to be considered as one of the possible risks we take. The problem with self-employment as a sole practitioner is that, should anything happen to you, there is no-one to keep the business going in your absence.

You will no doubt rarely consider such things as car accidents or chronic illness in your business plan, but Penny, a corporate coach, was involved in a serious train crash on her way to visit a client one day. This resulted not only in immediate hospitalisation, but long-term physiotherapy and difficulty in sitting down for anything other than short periods of time. It made running a coaching practice almost impossible and, sadly, Penny had not considered taking out any insurance to cover her loss of earnings.

We have tried to cover a wide range of possible reasons that a business might fail in order to help you consider these – and the many others you may be able to think of yourself – before you make any irreversible decisions that turn out not to be in your best interests.

You can see that a number of factors are involved in the provision of a successful practice. These include:

- Personal factors such as your own coaching skills, motivation and energy
- Financial factors, including not only the generation of sufficient income but the control of outgoings and the ability to keep accurate records on a regular basis
- Environmental factors such as location and ambience.

Reflection issues

- Think about the reasons why practices might fail. Do you believe any of these factors apply to you?
- Will you encounter family pressures? If so what might you do to ameliorate the situation?
- Location, location, location! This is what we usually hear from estate agents. Have you got a clearer idea about the pros and cons of the location you intend to use?

Having read this section, what issues in it do you believe that you need to address?

How will you do this?

Issue	Action	By when?	Done?

By tackling these issues, what results have you achieved?

If you have been unable to tackle any of the issues you have listed, what has prevented you?

What do you need to do to rectify the situation?

We have now looked at some of the pitfalls of running a small business, but what about the positive side of things? What are the special characteristics required to be a success? Let's take a look now at some of the traits that we hope you already have, or can perhaps acquire, in order to maximise your success.

The characteristics of success

We tend to think of people who give away corporate security to become self-employed as rather "devil-may-care" risk-takers but, in fact, the opposite is true. Qualities such as self-discipline and attention to detail are usually required for success. An amalgam of sensible risk-taking and good organisational skills will hold you in very good stead. Let us look at some of the personal factors that distinguish the successful from the less successful (Caird, 1993; Gordon, 1984).

Drive and self-motivation

Who makes the decisions about how to increase your client base? You do. Who makes decisions about how to balance your budget? You do. And who supervises you and prevents you from making serious errors of judgement? No-one. So personal motivation and drive are essential qualities. They mean you must want to succeed and be prepared to do whatever it takes work-wise to achieve this. People with drive and motivation are more likely to view obstacles and failures as challenges rather than as distressing setbacks. They are positive, optimistic thinkers, to whom it comes naturally to believe "I can" rather than "I cannot". You will need to believe in yourself and in your ability to provide services that clients will perceive as good value for money, and this self-belief may be something that you will personally need to work on.

Logical and creative thinking

As a coach, you may well say, "But this is already my forte!" If you are teaching it to others, then surely you have it in abundance yourself? Nonetheless, we all know of accountants who are hopeless at keeping their own financial affairs in order and hairdressers whose own hairstyle leaves a huge amount to be desired. So we need to ensure that you will apply this type of thinking to your own business.

The business pages of newspapers carry a great many stories of small business people who are hard working and forever optimistic, but that is not enough to stop them getting into difficulties.

Successful business people have the ability to look objectively and logically at their business, to be aware of their key priorities, to balance immediate needs and longer-term goals, to know when detail can be critical or just a distraction and to distinguish between the essential and the desirable. Looking ahead, planning for one year, three years, five years etc. may actually cause you completely to restructure your priorities for the immediate future.

Your ability to teach others to "think outside the box" and create alternative options is exactly what you need to turn around to apply to your creative business thinking. This enables you constantly to review your current policy or practice. Think of your business as a ball of plasticine that you are forever reshaping – it never sets, is always flexible and malleable, and you will find yourself playing with it constantly.

What looks good on paper or in theory may not work out as well in practice so, in exactly the same way that you will be encouraging clients to test out new ideas and activities, you are going to have to test out new ideas for your business. Good businesses are always testing new markets or new products, preferably before their competitors. Many of these come to nothing and you have probably noticed products that appear briefly on the supermarket shelves only to disappear again. Nonetheless, some will be very successful. If nothing is tried, nothing is gained. As American motivational speaker Michael Gelb once said: "If you want to double your success rate, you have to double your failure rate!" We refer you back to using risk assessment when you are experimenting, but many creative ideas have little downside beside perhaps some time wastage. Creative thinking can also involve coming to negative conclusions. Going out on a limb with an unusual advertising campaign might be money poorly spent compared to using your creativity to find a cheaper way of achieving the same result (getting an article written about your services in the local paper, for example).

Good leadership skills

Your role as a coach is going to require you to act, in a sense, as a team leader for clients, or, in the corporate sector, groups of clients. You will need to apply these same leadership skills to your business. How much leadership experience have you had? How good are you at making decisions where you have no-one else to defer to? How comfortable do you feel when you have taken a decision that carried risk? The ability to be your own leader is very important in self-employment.

Decision-making ability

One of the attributes of successful business people is that they seem able to make decisions that are both quickly taken and usually right. You will be making dozens of decisions, both big and small, every day and you will need to be able to do this with confidence and speed, as opposed to "humming and hawing" over a long period – and then still being uncertain about what you have decided. As your business develops, you simply will not have time to procrastinate, so do ensure that you constantly practise and hone this particular skill.

Reflection issues

- Are you logical and creative?
- Are you really motivated? Can you become more motivated?
- Measure your personal qualities against those of a successful businessperson. Which ones do you feel you have and which ones might you need to develop?

Having read this section, what issues in it do you believe that you need to address?

How will you do this?

Issue	Action	By when?	Done?

By tackling these issues, what results have you achieved?

If you have been unable to tackle any of the issues you have listed, what has prevented you?

What do you need to do to rectify the situation?

5

Business planning, and why it is crucial

Most successful businesses utilise business plans as a means of setting objectives for the organisation and subsequently as a yardstick against which to measure performance and forecasting ability. It is from these starting points that the organisation's budgets are derived – essentially sales income, cost of sales, overheads and profit – and woe betide the sales and marketing managers who get their forecasts wrong! Central and local governments go through similar processes at least once a year, sometimes with intermediate reviews and adjustments.

As an individual running your own business, all this might seem like using the proverbial sledgehammer to crack a nut – after all, is not your main concern just to make enough money to live on, pay the mortgage, perhaps run a car and have a few holidays? Unfortunately, life is rarely that simple. You may have family commitments, and to raise a child to adulthood (or beyond) can cost in the region of £100,000–£150,000. You may wish to retire at 60, 55 or even 50 and so may need to make large pension contributions to avoid relative poverty later on. Illness can strike at any time and deprive you of income. Then there is your professional development to consider – books, journals, courses, conferences, membership of professional bodies and so on. Such considerations should not be ignored. In a sense we are talking about your personal survival.

It can be difficult to separate your own personal require-ments from those of your business – after all, you are the business. Your own personal resources, skills and abilities make the business what it is. Your time is precious and should be utilised to achieve a balance between short-term, long-term and personal needs.

When planning your business it is helpful to have longer-term goals in mind. Do you want to work flat-out for 20 years and then retire or do something different? Or would you prefer a less pressured existence with, perhaps, greater variety in the type of work you do? Do you have such a choice? What personal constraints do you operate under? Will they always be there?

You and your business are unique. Although there may appear to be a certain common daily routine – issues such as seeing and helping clients and dealing with your administration and finances – nothing stays the same for very long. Professionally, you will change as your experience grows. Enormous advances in the scale and variety of tasks undertaken with electronic systems and equipment, for example, have already made and will continue to make an impact both on the potential efficiency of your business and on the sources, size and type of demand for your services.

It is not easy to project forward such trends to create a realistic scenario in which you may have to operate in, say, five or ten years' time and, however hard you try, you won't get it exactly right. Nonetheless, you should be aware of such developments and take account of them or make provision for them.

You may possibly remember that not so long ago many GPs operated as individuals without an appointment system – simply with a morning or afternoon "surgery" to which you turned up and waited. This was a very inefficient use of their time as well as the patients'. Now it seems almost inconceivable that anyone would operate in this way! What once seemed a revolutionary concept – for doctors to get together in a group practice to cover for each other and employ professional administrative support staff to maximise doctor/patient contact time – is now commonplace and expected. Being able to look forward and anticipate such possibilities is a helpful quality.

In the following sections, the processes involved in business planning will be described (Barrow, 2001). It should perhaps be emphasised that there is no single "golden" road to follow since all business plans should be geared to the circumstances, environment and resources prevailing for each business and to the nature and size of the potential market for its services. Nonetheless, there are common threads in the creation of any business plan.

Step 1. What business are you in?

A former management consultant said that his supervisor, when writing to a new client, would start a letter along the lines of "Dear Mr Mackay, you are in the (fish curing) business . . ." This sometimes produced a puzzled response from his clients but he was unrepentant, claiming that many people did not know what business they were in. If you are a follower of the stock market you may remember that large conglomerates – companies comprising many divergent businesses – were all the rage in the 1980s: Hanson, BTR, Grand Metropolitan and BATS for example. Now these companies have either sold off non-core activities or been taken over or merged. Vertical integration, i.e. control of production, distribution and sometimes retailing has also tended to gave way to horizontal integration, i.e. specialising in either the production, distribution or supply of goods and services to end users. The take-overs or mergers of banks, building societies, insurance companies, brewers, car manufacturers and communications companies have been particularly noticeable.

You may ask: "What has all this got to do with my coaching practice?" The answer lies in two parts.

First, both you and the chief executive of a multi-national company are constrained by time. In the course of a week you can give only limited consideration to a limited number of issues. If the issues are unrelated and call for different knowledge bases and skills then you will struggle to succeed. Second, it is much easier to build on existing strengths in knowledge and skills than to acquire new knowledge and/or skills. GPs can cover for each other and so can airline pilots but to mix them up could be catastrophic!

The same arguments may be applied to coaching. While you may well feel that you can assist clients no matter what their difficulties, the chances are that you will develop specialist areas – particularly if you go into a corporate setting – and this particular type of coaching will become your strength. You will certainly operate to your best abilities if you recognise your own limitations.

Of course, further specialised training and practical experience will expand skills and expertise but a realistic assessment of one's own capabilities is essential.

How far you go down the road of defining your business is a matter of personal choice. In your promotional literature or on your website you may wish to be quite specific about your particular expertise and the type of clients or companies that you assist (or have already assisted). You might argue that this may limit your clientele, but it does mean that you are probably excellent in your specialist area, and clients will come to you for that reason. If you needed a heart operation, you would, we are sure, prefer a cardiac specialist to a general surgeon, for example.

You may also wish to make a decision as to what other skills you develop, such as giving talks, teaching, writing articles, chapters or books, media work and supervising other coaches.

Some businesses have picked up on the American idea of a "mission statement" and you could, if you wished, use this to define your services:

> To ensure that you reach your full potential and beyond in
> the corporate environment, bringing benefit to yourself,
> your colleagues and your company.

Step 2. Defining your resources

A successful business is one that manages to optimise the use of its own resources to match the needs of its customers, and so it is worthwhile to list what these resources actually are. They may be personal (knowledge, skills, personal stamina) or environmental (geographical location, easy access for clients, lack of competition, pleasant environment and facilities etc.). None of these factors is usually represented on a balance sheet in monetary terms, though attempts are made from time to time in terms of goodwill (when a company is taken over at a higher value than its net assets) and the value of well-known brands.

A curriculum vitae (CV) is a useful starting point from which to extract information. The jobs you have held, qualifications attained, courses attended and your practical experience, all with the relevant dates, comprise the main elements. If you don't have a curriculum vitae, then produce one and update it periodically. A number of excellent books will help you do this including *Creating a Successful CV* by Simon Howard (1999). You may occasionally need a CV at short notice, particularly if you want to work within a corporate environment. Don't forget to include any registrations or accreditations. If you have written any articles or contributed to any publications, list them.

The purpose of a CV or its associate, your business plan, is to sell yourself as a credible supplier of those services you are offering. It is worth the effort to make it presentable and up to date.

The services you are offering come next. These should be described in easy-to-understand, non-technical terms. Referring to the TGROW model, for example, would be meaningless and confusing to the layperson. However, listing the most common types of specific assistance you give will be readily understood and helpful.

If you are offering face-to-face coaching services, the location of your practice in terms of convenient access and a pleasant and safe environment for potential clients is a resource to be listed. Of course, the day may come with cheap access to the internet and the use of on-line cameras when location ceases to have such relevance, but, unless you decide to undertake coaching via the telephone only, not yet.

Step 3. Define the potential demand for your services

Is there likely to be sufficient demand for your services? This is the fundamental question. To answer this question well involves a number of stages.

Stage 1

Bearing in mind realistic travelling distances or times, how big is your potential market: how many people in your catchment area are in a position to use your services? How many companies that you might offer your services to are located within travelling distance from your home? Will you be better served by considering predominantly telephone coaching?

As far as we know, no-one has yet done the necessary market research to determine how many people and organisations in the United Kingdom use professional coaching services in the course of a year and, of these, what share is served by private practitioners as opposed to major companies. Therefore, for the moment, common-sense calculations need to apply.

It is reasonable to expect a high correlation between the number of people with the ability to pay and the number of listed private practitioners. It is possible to attempt to be a little more precise. For example, the majority of clients are likely to be drawn from the AB socio-economic group (managers, administrative and professional people) comprising perhaps 20% of the population and, of these, most clients will be in the 20–40-year-old age group, comprising perhaps 30% of the population. Thus one could say there is a target group of around 6% of the general population.

Now, of course, all the above is very approximate. There will be some clients from other socio-economic groups such as C1 (skilled workers). Even within the AB group there will be some professions who use coaches more than others. One could also use a more typical age range of 25–50 years, and so on.

Stage 2

Until more research is done, there is little option but to do a calculation of the following type: Define your catchment area in terms of distance/time taken realistically for a client prepared to use your services. This could be 2–5 miles in a densely populated area with traffic problems or 10–30 miles in a rural district with clear roads or, in time terms, up to one hour.

Obtain the population figures for your catchment area. Local authority planning departments keep census figures. AA and Michelin guides also contain town populations.

Try to obtain the proportion of the catchment area population that is in the AB group. If this is not possible, compare the general wealth of the catchment area with other areas in terms of quality owner-occupied housing, new expensive cars, luxury shopping etc. and adjust an AB figure of 20% upwards or downwards accordingly.

Multiply the catchment area population by the AB percentage, e.g. 230,000 × 22% = 52,900. From local census figures, determine a typical client age group percentage: you might select ages 25–50, which might be 45% of the population. Multiply this figure by the catchment area AB population, e.g. 45% × 52,900 = 23,800. This last figure represents your target group.

Stage 3

Previous research (McMahon, 1994) suggested that a target group of 1,400 would support one counsellor or physiotherapist. On the assumption that a similar number of people would be required to support a coach then a target group of 23,800 people could, on average, support some 17 coaches. How many coaches are serving your catchment area? This is tricky, but you can adopt the following procedure.

Get together a list of coaches operating within your own catchment area and any surrounding areas together with their phone numbers and addresses. Many will advertise in the *Yellow Pages* and professional referral directories.

On a suitable large-scale map mark the location of each coach, including yourself. Draw a catchment area for each coach. You will now have a series of overlapping areas. Write down the proportion of each coach's area that overlaps your own. For example, those who live on the boundary of your area may draw 50% of their clients from your area. Those close to you may draw 80–90% from your area. Those who are a mile or so outside may draw 30% or so. Add together all the percentages and divide by 100.

This will give a rough indication of the number of coaches competing for the same target group of clients in your area. Compare this number with the number of coaches you have already calculated your catchment area would, on average, support. This will give an indication of whether competition for clients is likely to be high or low.

This is not the whole story. Established coaches with a good reputation can draw clients from greater distances, in the same way that out-of-town shopping centres can draw customers away from local shops. You may find that other coaches are specialising in different client groups from yourself. You may wish to consider contacting them to get an idea of how busy they are.

All of this is more important in the initial stages of planning and setting up your business. Once you start, you have already made a significant investment and you will find out soon enough if you have made a wise decision.

Assuming that you are satisfied there is sufficient potential demand for your services, you now have the problem of translating potential business into real business.

Step 4. Publicising your services

However excellent a coach you are, your expertise is unlikely to receive the recognition and reward it deserves unless you bring it to people's attention through advertising and publicity.

For the purposes of a business plan you do not need to go into great detail. More on this and on marketing generally is covered in later sections. However, you should decide how potential clients are to be made aware of your existence and your services. It helps if you know your catchment area well.

The following is a list of possible actions you can take:

- Let as many people as possible know that you are starting a coaching practice.
- Think of relatives or friends who may have contacts who may be potential clients.
- Take advice from other coaches as to the effectiveness of different forms of advertising.
- Put your name in relevant directories or registers. Remember that it can take a year before your advertisement may appear, as such directories are usually only published once a year.
- Advertise in the *Yellow Pages* or *Thomson Local* telephone directories (see www.thomweb.co.uk).
- Advertise in the local newspapers and free press.
- Circulate details to personnel managers in local authorities and organisations.
- Give talks to local clubs and societies.

- Join any local branch of your professional organisation.
- Issue local press releases.
- Take part in discussions or phone-ins on local radio stations.
- Write articles for local magazines and newspapers.
- Produce an information leaflet about yourself and your services.
- Ensure you have business cards available to give other professionals interested in your services.
- Create a website.

Some of these actions will cost money and you will need to budget for this accordingly. For example:

Adverts in directories and the media	£700
Postage	£80
Printing	£360
Telephone calls	£50
	£1190

Step 5. Business objectives and financial planning

At the end of the day, unless you have other forms of income or intend to run your practice as a sideline, you need to plan and feel confident that your income will exceed your expenses, including personal living expenses, pension contributions, taxes and investment in your business.

It is easy to overlook this last requirement but a frequent criticism of many traditional British manufacturers is their failure to spend money improving the skills of the workforce and replacing out-of-date and inefficient plant and equipment. Similarly, a coach operating from noisy, dingy premises with poor telephone connections and without the benefits of electronic equipment and systems will be at a disadvantage.

For many new businesses, the first major objective is to reach a break-even point – when income and expenditure are in balance – before running out of money. Some never make it and at the present time many of the internet-only companies, the so-called dot coms, are operating at a loss or have already gone out of business.

As a small businessperson, you should aim to have access to sufficient capital to last you well beyond your planned break-even point. One important purpose of a business plan can be to convince a bank manager, or whoever may make funds available, that you will be in profit and able to repay any loan within a reasonable time. How you do this is the subject of your short-term business plan objectives.

Short-term objectives are best illustrated by means of an example. Although the figures used are reasonably typical at the time of publication they will be different for each person. Suppose your objective is to break even within 12 months of starting the business. How do you plan, realistically, for this to happen?

Let us suppose you have done the previous exercises and satisfied yourself that there is sufficient potential demand for your services at the going fee rate and that you are ready to move on your advertising and publicity campaign. Let us also assume the following with regard to income and expenditures:

Income

You plan to charge a low fee of £25 per hour. You anticipate about two clients per week to start with, rising to about 20 per week after 12 months. You intend to take a week off at Easter and Christmas and also the whole month of August.

Expenditure

One-off expenditures

Advertising and publicity initially	£1,190
Furnishing and equipping office	£4,000
Holidays in August	£750
Christmas	£150
Training courses in October	£300
Accountant's fees after 12 months	£150
	£6,540

Average monthly business expenditures

Office rent	£200
Motor and travel	£80
Gas, electricity, water	£80
Telephone	£40
Supervision	£70
Insurance	£20
Books and journals	£20
National Insurance contributions	£20
Stationery, postage, minor items	£20
Ongoing advertising	£20
Subscriptions	£10
	£580

Living expenses monthly average

Rent/mortgage, pension contributions (£100 p.m.), food, clothes, entertainment, household bills etc.	£850
Total monthly expenses	£1,430

Now convert all of this into a table. Assume you start in January and project over two years: see Table 5.1.

As you can see from the table, not an encouraging example! At this rate you would be in your fourth year before you recovered your initial investment. Furthermore, you need to have some £12,000 in capital to avoid bankruptcy in August of Year 1. Would a bank loan help? Perhaps you decide you need £12,000 to cover the August in Year 1 and arrange to borrow this amount over two years with monthly repayments of £560. What would the first year look like now? See the results in Table 5.2.

There is no point in continuing. You are now bankrupt in May and are left owing the bank some 20 repayments totalling some £11,000. You may lose your car if you have one and possibly your home if you have put it up as security against the loan.

Table 5.1 Income and expenditure

Year 1: Month	Client sessions per month	Income (I)	Expenditure (E)	I – E	Cumulative surplus (+) or deficit (–)
January	8	200	6,620	–6,420	–6,420
February	16	400	1,430	–1,030	–7,450
March	24	600	1,430	–830	–8,280
April	24	600	1,430	–830	–9,110
May	40	1,000	1,430	–430	–9,540
June	48	1,200	1,430	–230	–9,770
July	56	1,400	1,430	–30	–9,800
August	–	–	2,180	–2,180	–11,980
September	72	1,800	1,430	+370	–11,610
October	80	2,000	1,730	+270	–11,340
November	88	2,200	1,430	+770	–10,570
December	66	1,650	1,580	+70	–10,500
		13,050	23,550		

Year 2: Month	Client sessions per month	Income (I)	Expenditure (E)	I – E	Cumulative surplus (+) or deficit (–)
January	88	2,200	1,430	+770	–9,730
February	88	2,200	1,580	+620	–9,110
March	88	2,200	1,430	+770	–8,340
April	66	1,650	1,430	+220	–8,120
May	88	2,200	1,430	+770	–7,350
June	88	2,200	1,430	+770	–6,580
July	88	2,200	1,430	+770	–5,810
August	–	–	2,180	–2,180	–7,990
September	88	2,200	1,430	+770	–7,220
October	88	2,200	1,730	+470	–6,750
November	88	2,200	1,430	+770	–5,980
December	66	1,650	1,580	+70	–5,910
		23,100	18,510		

Failure to calculate future cash flow and take action accordingly is a very common cause of bankruptcy. Now, it may well be possible to borrow a larger sum over a longer period, say £15,000 over five years or so, perhaps with a second mortgage. Again it would be essential to do a calculation along the lines shown above.

Table 5.2 Income and expenditure revised to include bank loan

Year 1: Month	Income (I)	Expenditure (E)	I – E	Capital left
January	12,200	7,180	5,020	+5,020
February	400	1,990	−1,590	+3,430
March	600	1,990	−1,390	+2,040
April	600	1,990	−1,390	+650
May	1,000	1,990	−990	−340
June	1,200	1,990	−790	−1,130

Note that although, technically, you were breaking even in the examples in the first year this was not enough to save the business unless you have sufficient capital of your own to see you past the point of maximum cash outflow.

At this point, you should be examining all your income and expenditure to see if you can improve the viability of your business. For example, you may decide the following:

Income

Start to see clients before you go "live", perhaps six per week in the evenings while remaining employed during the day. After 12 months of running the business and with extra training, raise fees to £30 per hour. Of course, still a lowish fee.

Expenditure

If possible, work from home and save £270 per month on rent, some contents insurance and most of the utilities bills. Put off pension contributions for two years or until you can afford them. Take only two weeks for a holiday in August and at no extra cost. But continue with your training and personal development.

Now, what would the first year's picture look like? As you can see from Table 5.3, our average monthly business expenditures have reduced to £310 per month from £580. Your personal living expenses have reduced to £750 per month from £850 and your client base starts with eight clients rather than two.

Clearly this is a much better situation. You have recovered your initial investment and income will improve further with a

Table 5.3 **Income and expenditure revised to reflect reduced costs**

Year 1: Month	Client sessions per month	Income (I)	Expenditure (E)	I – E	Cumulative surplus (+) or deficit (–)
January	32	800	6,250	–5,450	–5,450
February	40	1,000	1,060	–60	–5,510
March	48	1,200	1,060	+140	–5,370
April	42	1,050	1,060	–10	–5,380
May	64	1,600	1,060	+540	–4,840
June	72	1,800	1,060	+740	–4,100
July	80	2,000	1,060	+940	–3,160
August	44	1,100	1,060	+40	–3,120
September	88	2,200	1,060	+1,140	–1,980
October	88	2,200	1,360	+840	–1,140
November	88	2,200	1,060	+1,140	0
December	66	1,650	1,210	+440	+440
		18,800	18,360		

higher fee rate. You have to meet your accountant's bill but this should not be a problem. However, the taxman has his hand out and you cannot count your living expenses as tax deductible. More on this later but, just to complete the picture, a rough tax calculation (note that the following assumes your set-up costs are all tax deductible which may not be strictly correct):

Gross income	£18,800
Less set-up and business expenses	£9,360
£5,190 + (12 × £310) + £300 + £150 (accountant)	
	£9,440
Less personal allowance at time of writing	£4,745
Taxable income	£4,695
Tax @ 10% on £1,960	£ 196
Tax @ 22% on £2,735	£ 602
Tax payable	£ 798

You should have no difficulty meeting a tax bill of £800 that would probably be paid in two instalments.

As you should realise by now, short-term objectives are all about survival in the early stages of the business and cash flow is a crucial consideration. You also need to consider your longer-term objectives.

Although there are financial advantages to working from home, there are non-financial disadvantages, such as:

- Difficulty in separating work from home life.
- Insufficient space.
- Noise and potential disruption from other occupants.
- Difficulty maintaining a professional environment and image.

One objective therefore may be to find a suitable office/consulting room. As a new coach practitioner your fee rates will have to be competitive, since you have no reputation to justify anything more. However, you don't want to struggle to survive for years on end, seeing more clients than is good for you or for them.

A second objective may well be financial – to make sufficient surplus to keep client numbers at a manageable level, to invest in the business and your own personal development and to make pension contributions to permit a comfortable retirement.

A third objective may be to diversify away from a single business focus on coaching individual clients to perhaps working with groups, running courses or writing – all of these building on your own experience and expertise.

It is difficult at this stage to do realistic financial calculations extending over five years, say. However, let us suppose that following the more successful version of your first year you want to see what a second year might look like: this is shown in Table 5.4.

It looks as if pension contributions are now affordable and to make up for no contributions in Year 1, you could contribute, say, £200 per month. These are tax deductible provided they do not exceed the allowed percentage of your profit, but the new stakeholder pensions do allow up to £300 per month (less 22% contributed by HM government) irrespective of earnings.

Can you afford an office and the associated bills? Probably yes. Another, say, £300 per month is affordable and also tax deductible. Of course, you will have a sizeable tax bill since your

Table 5.4 **Income and revised expenditure in second year**

Year 2: Month	Client sessions per month	Income (I) (at £30 rate)	Expenditure (E)	I – E	Cumulative surplus (+) or deficit (–)
					B/F +440
January	88	2,640	1,710[1]	+930	+1,370
February	88	2,640	1,060	+1,580	+2,950
March	88	2,640	1,060	+1,580	+4,530
April	66	1,980	1,060	+920	+5,450
May	88	2,640	1,060	+1,580	+7,030
June	88	2,640	1,460[2]	+1180	+8,210
July	88	2,640	1,060	+1,580	+9,740
August	0	–	1,810[3]	–1,810	+7,980
September	88	2,640	1,060	+1,580	+9,560
October	88	2,640	1,360[4]	+1,280	+10,840
November	88	2,640	1,060	+1,580	+12,420
December	66	1,980	1,210[5]	+770	+13,190
		27,720			

[1] Tax of £400 paid and accountant's bill was £250 rather than £150.
[2] Second tax instalment paid.
[3] You decided to take August off (holidays £750) because of improved finances.
[4] Training course, cost £300.
[5] Christmas cost £150

income is higher and your allowable expenditures are lower. For example:

Gross income	£27,720
Less business expenditure	£4,270
12 × £310 + £250 + £300	
	£23,450
Less personal allowance*	£4,745
Taxable income	£18,705
Tax @ 10% on £1,960*	£196
Tax @ 22% on £16,745*	£3,684
Tax payable	£3,880

* When you read this, taxes will have changed so you need to insert the current rates and allowances.

Nonetheless, you do have the cash to pay your tax and should you start making pension contributions and renting an office in Year 3, your tax would reduce by some £1,240 if your income remained at the above level.

Business administration

This is an often neglected but important part of any business. People, particularly politicians, tend to use the word "bureaucracy" in a negative sense as if it was something undesirable and yet it is efficient bureaucracy that makes everything work. Answering telephones, dealing with correspondence and messages, keeping good records and files, ordering goods, keeping stocks, dealing with money matters, housekeeping and organising things generally all play a part.

As far as a business plan is concerned, perhaps the most important things to list are the separation of your business bank account from your personal bank account, the method by which your clients pay and how you intend to keep financial records and make provision for tax. We return to these matters later.

Summary of points for a business plan

- Define the business you are (or intend to be) in.
- Define your resources.
- Define the potential demand for your services.
- Decide how you would publicise your services.
- Decide your business objectives and plan your finances.
- Decide the main aspects of your business administration.

Now, if you still want to continue, do your own business plan, show it to someone who is familiar with the concept and get some feedback. Banks offer an excellent service vetting business plans. Would it be credible to someone in a position to lend you money? Even more important – is it credible to you?

Reflection issues

- What are your business objectives? Are they realistic?
- What demand do you think there will be for your services?

Would a charge fee of £60 per hour be worth the risk and still bring in sufficient business?
* Does undertaking any of these exercises deter you? If so, what might that say about your attitude towards self-employment?

Having read this section, what issues in it do you believe that you need to address?

How will you do this?

Issue	Action	By when?	Done?

By tackling these issues, what results have you achieved?

If you have been unable to tackle any of the issues you have listed, what has prevented you?

What do you need to do to rectify the situation?

6

Business essentials

Reducing financial risks

Most of us, in our personal lives, try to minimise possible financial losses by taking out hefty insurance policies. In fact, it is hard to purchase much these days, particularly in the electrical goods market, and get away without purchasing some sort of extended warranty. These are usually straightforward decisions based on simple likelihood: if the iron packs up, is it worth paying £20 p.a. insurance when irons rarely do pack up and only cost about that to replace in any event? If we are uninsured and have a car accident however – which, over a lifetime, is quite likely – we may lose our home to pay the costs of the other party, if the accident is our fault.

In business, the assessment of risks is far more complex and cannot be dealt with simply by taking out an insurance policy. Who is going to insure you against your business failing? Risk taking in business is a much more complex process as it is not always possible to "cover oneself" and one simply has to assess and then, possibly, manage the risk. Sometimes the greatest risk is to do nothing (the saying "To risk nothing is to risk everything" can be very accurate), but sometimes the greater risk is to tinker with a perfectly good business. Newly appointed chief executives can be prone to this when they perceive a need to stamp their personal mark by restructuring, out-sourcing or adopting the latest fashionable management techniques.

Good businesses can become out-dated or undermined by competitors. Those that acquire and, more importantly, are able to apply cutting-edge knowledge can secure a premium for their services. This is probably one of the most important points to bear in mind when running your own business. The importance of moving forward constantly and staying up-to-date or even ahead of the game is vital. Large companies often employ staff simply to work on change management, and to ensure that individuals within the company are constantly managing and incorporating change into their work.

Do you see yourself as a risk taker? Willingness to take risks is very much an individual characteristic – top sports-people almost always have it, for example. However, the end result is invariably improved by careful analysis and good judgement. Fallback positions if things go wrong need to be determined in advance to prevent hastily made and wrong reactions under pressure. It is a mark of a successful person to know when to cut one's losses and get out rather than persist with a lost cause. However, identifying at which point to do this is one of the most difficult decisions, and many businesses lose everything simply because they left that option until it was too late.

Running a coaching business should not be a particular gamble, but neither should the business be allowed to stagnate for a lack of willingness to take managed risks and make sensible decisions.

As success beckons, never rest on your laurels. One or two major British retailers have been in the news in the last few years for this failing, and it has been a very expensive one. It is a sad fact that it takes a long time to build a reputation for good value products or services but only a short time to lose it.

The successful businessperson realises that continued success depends on on-going and objective appraisal of the business and current market forces. Success provides the opportunity, in terms of time and resources, not to sit back, but to plan and implement improvements for still further success.

Business knowledge and skills

The chapter on why businesses fail provided a number of examples of people who may have been good coaches but, because they lacked basic business knowledge and skills, were unable to succeed in developing their practice. We therefore cannot overestimate the importance of acquiring these skills and using them seriously and conscientiously.

Planning, organising and attention to detail

We have discussed at length and in detail the importance of business planning. It is important in that it provides a means of measuring how good you are at forecasting and providing a structure to your business. When plans fail, in one respect or another, the reasons for failure are thus usually fairly clear. This means that lessons can be learned, adjustments made and, hopefully, techniques and decisions improved.

It is extraordinary that people go to immense lengths to plan holidays and expeditions lasting just weeks or months to the nth degree, and yet will start up a business without giving it anywhere near the same detailed forethought.

We appreciate that running a one-person coaching practice does not involve the level of risk and decision-making of large companies, but nonetheless, to succeed, the same principles of planning, organising and attention to detail still apply. Opportunities need to be taken. The best use must be made of the resources available to you. Reserves, in the form of savings or overdraft facilities, and time in the form of extra hours working, may sometimes need to be drawn upon. Successes need to be consolidated and built upon ready for any further expansion you wish to undertake.

Using the help available

It is always a good idea to think, ahead of time, of whom you might be able to call on to give you extra help with the various aspects of business life that may crop up when you are working alone. However confident you are, no-one can predict quite when, or for what reason, you will need to call on assistance, so spend a little time thinking through who will be there to help you if you need it. You may also need advice from time to time – whom can you call on to give you that?

Let's take a look at who is around for you . . .

Other coaches

During your researches, you may well have come across others offering coaching services, and as long as you are not in direct competition with each other, exchanging information can be very useful. Other coaches may tell you such things as what fee levels may be charged, what sort of clients they have and how far clients are prepared to travel. They may share ideas about their successes (and failures) in attracting clients. If they are very successful, they may even agree to refer surplus clients to you on the basis that one day you may be in a position to return the favour. There is also the further possibility that, at some future date, joining your practices together may be in your best interests. If there is one in the area, it is helpful to join a professional support group where you can meet others to discuss your experiences and problems.

Friends and family

Personal support can be as important as financial support, and having a partner and/or other close family around you who support and understand your hopes and dreams will make a big difference to you.

If you are lucky, you may have friends who would be willing to step in and help you in the initial stages of setting up your business – perhaps they may develop your advertising materials, or the friend is a computer wizard who may design your letterheads. Look around you and consider who might be willing to step in in an emergency (even to man the phone line, for example). Good friends and close family are usually only too happy to help, as they know that you will offer support to them if they also need it.

Banks

Banks want to lend you money if they possibly can – they stay in business by lending money for profit. Therefore banks are a good resource to look at your business plan very closely. In fact, some banks provide business plan templates on a PC disc so that you can complete the relevant sections. Microsoft's PowerPoint software also has a business template. It focusses you on the key aspects of your proposed business and looks professional when you give a presentation.

The business adviser at your local branch should be able to appraise and assess your business proposals objectively and give you good advice. Your local bank is likely to have many small businesses as clients – possibly even one or two coaches with their own practices – and may well have a view as to the viability of your proposals, should you need a loan or overdraft. If you do need to borrow money to finance your business in the early stages, then you may wish to discuss with your adviser the cheapest methods, including overdraft facilities or loans. An unauthorised overdraft should be avoided as this can be costly. We have known some "entrepreneurs" who raised money by using just their credit cards. This can be more expensive than the unauthorised overdrafts! If you do borrow, it is very important that you make sure you earmark the money for specific business purposes.

Obtain alternative quotes and conditions, as your own bank may not be the most competitive. You will need to show your business plan in support of your proposal, so ensure that you have this ready before you approach a bank.

Banks have come in for much criticism recently – overcharging, incompetence, bankrupting small businesses unnecessarily and being indifferent and unresponsive to complaints, the list goes on. Like politicians, they tend to respect only those who wield similar levels of power. It has been said that if you owe a bank £1,000 it can make your life a misery but if you owe it £10 million you will receive courteous attention!

However, the high street banks do have a range of services available to help small businesses and we would not wish to say that they cannot be very helpful to you. For example, they can provide free financial software and a range of leaflets, booklets and books on a range of issues relating to self-employment, as well as specialist staff able to help you design your business.

Accountants

It is possible to do without the services of an accountant if your income is below £15,000 a year. If this is the case then you can prepare your own accounts and send these in to the Inland Revenue. This will save you money. However, you will not then get the benefit of an accountant's up-to-date knowledge of tax breaks. Therefore we believe that employing an accountant to compile your end-of-year accounts is strongly advisable. This is even more important if you wish to obtain a mortgage or sizeable business loan in the future.

As a prospective client, an initial meeting (preferably with someone personally recommended) is likely to cost you very little – possibly nothing at all. However, the accountant can usually provide helpful advice on setting up your own business, for example:

- The different headings under which to record your expenditure
- What expenditures are allowable for tax purposes and whether they are fully claimable in the current year or written down over a number of years
- The financial records you need to keep
- The use of bank or building society accounts for income, expenditure and making provision for tax
- The pros and cons of using an online bank account.

Although most of these subjects are covered later, tax regulations can and do change and accountants are obliged to keep up to date. In addition to preparing your accounts, with the advent of self-assessment in relation to taxation an accountant can also complete the relevant documentation from the Inland Revenue on your behalf from the information you provide.

When you delve a little deeper into finding a suitable accountant you will soon realise that there are different types with different professional accountancy qualifications. There are chartered accountants, management accountants, incorporated financial accountants, international accountants and so on. They are normally members of established professional accountancy bodies. Chartered accountants are usually considered to be the highest level in the profession in the UK and normally the Inland Revenue, banks and building societies will accept the accounts they produce for their purposes. However, other accountants may also be qualified to undertake your work although they may not be able to undertake a full company audit.

Government-funded initiatives

Depending on your age and the location of your business, there may be schemes (such as the Prince's Youth Business Trust for the under 30s) and local funds available for your business start-up, if this might be of interest to you.

Additionally, at local level, various initiatives exist to promote small business start-up and entrepreneurship in general. In some cities, specialised agencies have been set up to attract investment resources (grants, bank loans etc.), which are used to support all small enterprises. These agencies are comparable to investment trusts. Some local authorities also provide special refurbishment grants to small enterprises wanting to upgrade their premises.

Business Link is a national business advice service that provides information on all business needs and access to a wide network of business support organisations. Its website provides useful information and guidance and is well worth a visit: http://www.businesslink.gov.uk

Enterprise agencies exist to encourage new business and details can be obtained from your local reference library. Successive governments have been criticised for making life difficult for small businesses and the recent bringing forward in time of tax payments supports this view in spite of rhetoric to the contrary. However, enterprise agencies funded by both public and private sources can be helpful and frequently provide a free advice service. If you have been unemployed for three months but have some start-up capital, you may be eligible for an "enterprise allowance" which comprises one year of weekly payments.

You can get further details on these and other such services by contacting your local authority, job centre or the Department of Trade and Industry.

Educational institutes, local councils, libraries etc.

If the business side of running your own practice is not your strong point, then you may find some useful courses run by your local authority's further education institutes, such as in bookkeeping and accounting, marketing, communications and publicity. Day or evening classes are frequently available and details can be obtained from your town hall or local library.

Some local authorities have an Economic Development Department or, at least, officers who are concerned with reducing unemployment levels in the borough, who tend to work in association with agencies and employers. Government grants are often given to development agencies, particularly to regenerate previously deprived areas. Some local authorities own business premises that are available for rent, usually for less than a private sector let.

As a coach, your business will depend on your being able to attract significant numbers of clients able to pay your fees. One advantage of this career is that you can develop coaching via telephone, so the location of your clients will not be so important. However, you will no doubt wish to offer face-to-face appointments as well. While it is not too difficult to assess the general level of wealth in your catchment area from the proportion of good quality privately owned houses, shops, cars etc., the census statistics held by local planning departments (available for a fee) provide a breakdown of the various socio-economic groups.

The reality of your coaching practice is that your clients must to be able to afford your fees if you are to be able to make an income.

Reflection issues

- What type of help might you need?
- Where can you get the help from?
- What help might you be able to offer others in return?

Having read this section, what issues in it do you believe that you need to address?

How will you do this?

Issue	Action	By when?	Done?

By tackling these issues, what results have you achieved?

If you have been unable to tackle any of the issues you have listed, what has prevented you?

What do you need to do to rectify the situation?

PART 3

Money matters

7

Basic finance

In the many talks that one of the authors has given on private practice, financial matters don't seem to evoke the same interest and enthusiasm as other topics. No doubt, if all coaches had the unpaid services of a trained book-keeper or accountant, the tasks of collecting fees, accounting for expenditures and generally helping to keep the practice on a sound financial footing would be very happily delegated. Unfortunately, this is not the case and even book-keepers are obliged to make a living by charging for their services.

In any event, it does not pay to be too dependent on the services of others. A contact in the medical profession relied totally on her accountant and after a few years found herself owing the Inland Revenue £75,000 because the accountant had taken advantage of this dependence.

It might seem unfair, but if your accountant, your solicitor, your surveyor, your estate agent or even your GP or dentist gets it wrong, it is you who has to live with the consequences.

Keeping your finances in good order is more a matter of self-discipline and common sense than one of financial expertise (see Truman, 1997). So what's involved?

Let us consider Mr Micawber's problem from Charles Dickens' *David Copperfield*:

Annual income twenty pounds, annual expenditure nineteen nineteen six, result happiness.

Annual income twenty pounds, annual expenditure twenty pounds ought and six, result misery.

Fortunately for Mr Micawber, he and his hungry family were able to emigrate to Australia, where his wisdom and talents were rewarded.

The problem, which we have already met in the business plan section, is that of cash flow. If your expenditures exceed your financial ability to pay, then you are in debt and if the problem persists you will be bankrupt and risk having your assets seized to pay off your creditors. Note that we used the term "financial ability to pay" rather than "income". The term "financial resources" could also be used. Nearly every business starts off by spending more money than it earns. A business survives this difficult period if:

- It has sufficient capital of its own to see it through the period of negative cash flow (i.e. when expenditure is greater than income), or
- It can borrow sufficient capital to do this, or
- It can issue shares in exchange for sufficient capital.

The last option is not really applicable to a private practice unless it is turned into a company and complies with all the necessary requirements of company law.

As a follow-up to the cash flow exercise undertaken earlier, let us consider the following case:

- You borrow £15,000 over five years with monthly repayments of £375.
- You start with eight client sessions in January at £25 per session rising by eight sessions each month except when you take holidays, where the income is reduced pro-rata to the amount of holiday taken.
- You spend an extra £500 in August on a holiday of two weeks in Year 1.
- You also take a week off in April and December of both Year 1 and Year 2.
- You spend £300 on training courses in October of Year 1 and Year 2.
- You spend an extra £250 at Christmas in Year 1 and Year 2.
- You get your office redecorated and recarpeted in January of Year 2 at a cost of £1,000.

- You take off the whole of August in Year 2 and spend an extra £1,000.
- You pay your accountant's bill of £350 in February of Year 2.
- You increase your fees to £30 per session for new clients only in January of Year 2.
- Eight existing client sessions per month are replaced by eight new client sessions throughout Year 2 except as affected by holidays.
- You do not exceed 88 client sessions in a month. Your average business expenditure, excluding the loan repayments, is £600 per month (includes office rent of £200 per month).
- Your personal allowance (known as drawings) is £900 per month (which includes £200 per month pension contribution in Year 2).
- You have an additional start-up cost of £4,000 incurred in the first month.

Now do the following exercise! Lay out a table (which has been started off for you in Table 7.1) as follows. Work out the cumulative cash flow (or bank balance) for the first 24 months.

Do you make it or go under?

When you have completed your own table, check it against Table 7.2. Don't worry if there are a few minor differences. No one can forecast this accurately anyway.

Comments

Although, technically, you run out of cash in August of Year 2, it is only by some £120 and this could be managed by deferring expenditures until September, borrowing from a friend, seeing a few more clients in June or July etc. Alternatively you may have an overdraft facility at the bank or be able to pay from your own resources.

You may notice that no provision has been made for tax. In Year 1 you just about break even as far as the taxman is concerned, since business expenditure of £11,500 added to loan interest of about £2,000 more or less balances your income of £13,850. It might in fact be worth making your missing first year's pension contributions in January of Year 2 so that these can be offset against your Year 2's profit.

Table 7.1 Cumulative cash flow: first few months

Month	Client sessions per month	Income	Business expenditure	Loan repayment	Drawings	Total outgoings	Cash flow	Bank balance
January	8	(15,000+) 200	4,600	375	900	5,875	+9,325	+9,325
February	16	400	600	375	900	1,875	−1,475	+7,850
March	24	600	600	375	900	1,875	−1,275	+6,575
April	24	600	600	375	900	1,875	−1,275	+5,300
May	40	1,000	600	375	900	1,875	−875	+4,425

Table 7.2 Cumulative cash flow: first two years

Year 1: Month	Income	Business expenditure	Loan repayment	Drawings	Total outgoings	Cash flow	Bank balance
January	(15,000) + 200	4,600	375	900	5,875	+9,325	+9,325
February	400	600	375	900	1,875	−1,475	+7,850
March	600	600	375	900	1,875	−1,275	+6,575
April	600	600	375	900	1,875	−1,275	+5,300
May	1,000	600	375	900	1,875	−875	+4,425
June	1,200	600	375	900	1,875	−675	+3,750
July	1,400	600	375	900	1,875	−475	+3,275
August	800	600	375	1,400	2,375	−1,575	+1,700
September	1,800	600	375	900	1,875	−75	+1,425
October	2,000	900	375	900	2,175	−175	+1,450
November	2,200	600	375	900	1,875	+325	+1,775
December	1,650	600	375	1,150	2,125	−475	+1,300
	13,850	11,500	4,500	11,550			

Table 7.2 (continued)

Year 2: Month	Income	Business expenditure	Loan repayment	Drawings	Total outgoings	Cash flow	Bank balance
January	2,240 [1]	1,600	375	900	2,875	−635	+665
February	2,280 [2]	950	375	900	2,225	+55	+720
March	2,320	600	375	900	1,875	+445	+1,165
April	1,770	600	375	900	1,875	−105	+1,060
May	2,400	600	375	900	1,875	+525	+1,585
June	2,440	600	375	900	1,875	+565	+2,150
July	2,480	600	375	900	1,875	+605	+2,755
August	–	600	375	1,900	2,875	−2,875	−120
September	2,560	600	375	900	1,875	+685	+565
October	2,600	900	375	900	2,175	+425	+990
November	2,640	600	375	900	1,875	+765	+1,755
December	2,010	600	375	1,150	2,125	−115	+1,640
	25,740	8,850	4,500	12,050			

[1] 80 client sessions @ £25, 8 @ £30 = £2,240
[2] 72 client sessions @ £25, 16 @ £30 = £2,280

It is only when you do an exercise of this sort that you are able to foresee problems before they arrive. The last problem you need is an unauthorised overdraft and your bank manager threatening to call in your loan.

Notice also the "double whammy" of taking a holiday – no income but higher expenditure. No provision has been made for illness, but to be on the safe side, you should perhaps budget for, say, two weeks of illness when you are unable to see clients in the year.

Again, we have assumed that your set-up expenses are tax deductible. In reality, depending upon your situation, certain building costs and purchases may receive a capital allowance and are not tax deductible in the usual sense. An accountant's advice would clarify this.

Having assured yourself that, on paper at least, you have a viable business, you now need to set up systems to monitor and control your finances. This is important. It won't work through optimism and wishful thinking alone.

8

Systems and administrative principles

We hope you don't shudder at these words. Some people do. But much is straightforward and just requires the daily discipline to do it.

Separate business from personal finance

First of all, separate as far as possible your business income and expenditure from your personal income and expenditure. If you don't do this you'll get into a dreadful mess and pay a heavy price when you come to year end and have to submit your books and records for inspection by your auditor.

The easiest way of doing this is to keep a separate bank or building society account for all your business financial transactions. Of course, sometimes you have to pay cash out of your own pocket – taxis, parking fees etc. – and sometimes you may use a personal credit or debit card. Always ask for and keep a receipt. It is easy to forget when you're just buying a dozen stamps, but it all adds up.

Record income and expenditure

Keep a day book (more on this later) in which to record each item of income, the day it was received, whom it was from, the cheque number if paid by cheque and the type of service paid for. In the same book, but on the facing page, record each item of expenditure. Use separate columns for cheque payments and cash or personal payments. Again, record the date, the cheque number, whom the payment was made to and the type of expenditure, e.g. stationery, travel, office rent etc.

At the end of each month, total up your income and expenditure. Work out roughly how much you can afford to pay yourself and how much you should put aside for the inevitable tax demand. Use a new page for each month.

The day book logs your daily income and expenditure and is a primary source of data for your accounts (see the example in Table 8.1).

Finally, carry out reconciliation. You can't do this until you have your month's bank statement, which may contain items not recorded in the day book such as standing orders for National Insurance payments, direct debits, standing orders or pension contributions and charges made or interest paid by the bank. This can be a tricky exercise that is covered later in detail.

Keep a separate record of expenditure by type. You will need a second and separate cash book to log all expenditures under appropriate headings – telephone and fax bills, motor and travel, advertising and publicity etc. You will need a book with, perhaps, 20 columns. It is best to enter all the details from your day book under the appropriate heading on a monthly basis. At year-end, total up all expenditures under each heading. Your accountant/auditor will need this to prepare your profit and loss account.

You can use a hardback book with about 20 columns extending over a double page to keep the expenditure record. It could look something like Table 8.2 but with more headings. Start a new month on a new page.

Variations

If you have a good financial accounting package on your personal computer then you may need to enter data just once and usually the software will undertake reconciliation and throw out discrepancies for you to resolve. These systems can work out the VAT payable too. However, do not expect perfection. The old saying "garbage in, garbage out" (GIGO) applies to all computer systems.

Bank cheque or current accounts tend to pay very low interest rates, sometimes as little as 0.1%, even on a balance of several thousand pounds. At the same time you will be charged a hefty fee if you overdraw on your business account without

Table 8.1 Day book

Month: August 2000

Income (left hand page)

Date	Description	Type	Cheque No.	£
1/8/00	J Jaques	Client	0071	30.00
1/8/00	S Jones	Client	5641	30.00
3/8/00	P Loi	Client		30.00
2/8/00	J Marie	Client	0988	30.00
4/8/00	Peter Jay	Client	0911	30.00
		Totals		

Expenditure (right hand page)

Date	Description	Cheque No.	Bank	Cash
2/8/00	Postage			4.39
3/8/00	Gas bill	0091	26.20	
3/8/00	Rymans	0092	34.99	
4/8/00	National Rail	0093	22.00	
	Stationery			5.30
		Totals		

Table 8.2 Expenditure record

August 2000 Date Item		Capital items	Premises costs	Postage, stationery etc	Travel and motor	Total
2/8	Postage			4.39		4.39
2/8	Gas bill		26.20			26.20
2/8	Stationery			34.99		34.99
4/8	Travel				22.00	22.00
4/8	Taxis				5.30	5.30
Total for August						
Brought forward July						
Carried forward Sept						

authorisation. A way around this is to make arrangements with the bank to have two accounts. The chequebook or paying out account is used to receive all income and pay all expenditures with a permanent balance being maintained of, say, £500. The other account or paying in account holds all excess funds over £500 and tops up funds from the cheque book account – and, more importantly, pays a more reasonable interest rate. Monitor this paying in account carefully every month. Alternatively, you could use a chequebook account with a building society but if there are a lot of transactions they may be reluctant, since you are obviously running a business and involving them in the costs of processing your cheques and standing orders.

Fee collection

There is nothing to beat being paid on time. Therefore, we would advise that clients pay by cash or cheque at the end of each session. Monthly invoicing of private clients will inevitably mean that some clients will disappear owing you a month's money. You have to ask yourself whether your cash flow can take that risk.

The way you prefer your clients to pay – cash at the time of the session, invoicing after a number of sessions etc. – will be personal to you. However, ensuring that payment is made in good time is essential when your livelihood depends on this.

Even when dealing with organisations that require an invoice, have the invoice prepared in advance and post it the same day. Your survival may depend on prompt payment. It can be helpful to check with the organisation in advance what payment policies are in place. For example, although you can encourage organisations to pay promptly you cannot enforce payment. One local authority used to pay within 30 days as individual housing managers had control over payments. A change in policy meant that all monies were paid centrally and the payment time went from 30 to 90 days. No amount of telephone calls or letters speeded up the payment process. In addition, chasing payments requires time and energy. The reality in this case came down to the fact that if you wanted the work you had to accept the payment terms, and if you did not then someone else would.

You can outline your payment policy in your terms and conditions of business, which form part of your contract with the individual client or organisation. More consideration is given to fees later in the book.

Make provision every month for income tax

We recommend opening a separate tax saving account. Choose one with a good interest rate and reasonably quick access. Normally you will get a reasonable period of notice of how much tax you owe and by when it should be paid. This way, you won't be caught owing money you have not got and you will get interest as well – net of tax, of course. However, it is important to remember that due to changes in the taxation system tax is now paid ahead of time in two annual instalments, usually January and July of each year (Whitely, 2002). Inland Revenue staff are always prepared to help with any enquiries.

Income

Pay the monies you receive into your business account via your paying-in book every few days. After entering all the details into your day book, write the name of the person and the amount on your paying-in stub so you can track the monies you have paid in and write your account number on the back of all cheques being paid in. This way you reduce the possibility of cheques going astray. Normally the bank will credit your payments on the same day, provided you bank before their close-off time, which might be 4pm. However, as you will be aware, you cannot draw cash against the cheques until they have cleared, normally some three to four working days later, and longer if you choose an account with an ex-building society which uses the services of a clearing bank.

It is straightforward to check your bank statement against your paying-in book. Sometimes there will be differences. You may have forgotten to list all the cheques or may have added them up incorrectly. Sort these out straight away. You may also have non-cheque income paid directly into your account, including bank interest. This form of payment is becoming more popular with a range of organisations and can be in your interests as it speeds up the payment process. You will come across the term BACS (Banks Automated Clearing System), which is the most popular form of this type of payment. It is usual for organisations paying in this way to send you a note of the amount being paid and the date it is due to be paid into your bank account.

Expenditure

Your bank statement will generally not tally against the cheques you have written that month for a number of reasons:

- Cheques you have written in previous months may not be presented or even cleared until the present month.
- Cheques written in the current month may not be presented or cleared until future months.
- You may have a number of non-cheque items such as bank charges and standing orders or direct debits for items such as National Insurance, pension contributions, subscriptions, rent, utilities charges etc.

As for income, check the validity of all entries when you get your statement. If you close off your books at the end of each month, make sure your bank gives you a statement for the same period. Banks try to spread production of statements to avoid the month-end peak but if you are paying for their services there is no reason for you to go along with this. It is easier to reconcile your books and bank statements if there is a degree of consistency in the accounting period.

Keep a record of expenditure by type

Just as a company keeps a separate account of its expenditures on raw materials, employee wages and salaries, rents and utilities costs etc., so you will also need to do the same, but on a more simplified scale. Apart from being useful from a monitoring and control point of view, your accountant will need the information to prepare your profit and loss account and balance sheet for submission to the Inland Revenue and for the assessment of your income tax liability. If you don't keep a record, your accountant will have to do it using your day book and bank statements and this will increase his/her charges massively.

Capital items

This covers all items that have a significant life, a significant cost and form part of the physical assets of the business, such as motorised transport, equipment (computers, fax machines, photocopiers etc.), furniture and significant furnishings. These are kept separate because their cost is generally not 100% allowable against profits in the year they were acquired, although there maybe some exceptions.

With capital items, the cost is spread over the nominal life of the asset. For example, if you acquire a second-hand car for £5,000 for business purposes, this may be "written down" or depreciated over five years, say, with £1,000 per year being charged to the costs of the business.

Note that the rules used do not represent reality. An asset may have a longer or shorter life in practice and it may have a residual value when it is disposed of. Your accountant will know the rules used by the Inland Revenue and be able to make the necessary adjustments.

Premises costs

This item covers rent, cleaning, repairs, redecoration and generally any work required to keep your business premises in good order. It also includes charges for gas, electricity and water and any rates or taxes levied on the premises.

If you are operating from a room in your home, then only a proportion of these costs is allowable, typically about a third. Again, an accountant's advice is helpful on this.

Postage, printing, stationery and minor office items and consumables

These items are self-explanatory.

Telephone and fax bills

These can include telephone charges for internet use and the use of mobile phones as well as standard landlines. Emails and text messaging via mobile phones are becoming increasingly popular and your overall costs can be quite substantial – £1,000 in a year would not be unusual. These costs are easier to justify if you have dedicated lines for business use. If your business shares a domestic line there is the problem of untangling business from personal or family use.

Publications and journals

All published material necessary to keep you up to date or to assist you directly in your business is an allowable expense.

Advertising, promotion and publicity

This would include advertisements in the *Yellow Pages*, *Thomson Local Directory*, professional directories, newspapers and on the internet, and also the costs of any event or website used directly to promote your business.

Seminars and conferences

Record the cost of all activities, apart from basic training, designed to improve your professional competence.

Professional consultancy

Costs of courses/registrations that allow you to retain your professional credentials are an allowable expense.

Professional subscriptions

This includes the cost of belonging to all relevant associations, societies or organisations in connection with your business, including the costs of publications regularly subscribed to (avoid double-count with seminars and conferences above).

Motor and travel

This item includes the costs of licensing, repairing, running, hiring and insuring any motorised vehicle used exclusively for your business (but not the purchase cost, which is a capital item). If the vehicle is also used for personal or social reasons, then only the business proportion is claimable as an expense. Other travel costs – plane, train, bus, taxi, hotel etc. – are also allowable.

Insurance

This includes professional indemnity insurance and your office contents insurance.

Bank charges

These are self-explanatory.

Accountant/auditor fees

These are self-explanatory.

National Insurance contributions

These are a no-choice business expense but are not allowable for tax relief, except for those of your employees. Keep a record to balance the books.

Pension contributions

Strictly speaking, these are not a business expense but are allowable for tax relief (can you reconcile the logic with the National Insurance above?) subject to the age/net income percentages laid down by the Inland Revenue.

Drawings

Although not strictly a business expense, you should record all monies you pay yourself from the business, including money you put aside to provide for your income tax liability. Your accountant will also need to know the amount (though can probably deduce it) to prepare your balance sheet.

It is worth noting that your income tax liability, though, is not based on what you draw from the business (unlike a wage or salary) but on a calculated profit – business income minus business expenditure minus depreciation minus allowable pension contributions. So even if you drew nothing and lived on fresh air, you could still have a potential income tax liability. As Mark Twain wryly observed, "In this life you can be certain of two things – that one day you will die and that there will be taxes." In reality, your own personal income will be highly correlated with your profits unless you are either running down the business or making substantial investments in it.

Calculating your tax

At the end of each month you can use your day book entries to calculate your monthly income and expenditure, how much you can afford to pay yourself and how much to set aside for tax. For example:

Cheque income	1,530.00
Cash income	70.00
Direct payments into bank	425.00
Total income	2,025.00
Cheque expenditure	321.21
(capital expenditure excluded)	
Cash expenditure	72.99
(capital expenditures excluded)	
Direct debits and standing orders	256.34
(excluding National Insurance,	
but including pension contributions)	
Total expenditure	650.54
Notional profit	1,374.46
Taxable income	979.04
(profit – $^1/_{12}$ personal allowance of 4,745.00)	
Tax @ 10% on $^1/_{12}$ of 1,960.00 (163.33)	16.33
Tax @ 22% on residue (979.04 – 163.33)	179.46
Provision for tax	195.79
Can pay myself	1,178.67
(1,374.46 – 195.79)	

Although we have shown the calculation to the nearest penny, this is not necessary and at current tax rates it is probably simpler to put aside 20% of your notional profit. It is your money and it does not hurt to over-provide and obtain some interest in the meantime.

You may also note that we have not included any capital expenditure in the calculation or any depreciation allowance arising from this. Again, this will result in an over-provision for tax but we imagine you would prefer to have more money in an interest-bearing tax account than is strictly needed. There is no problem in spending any excess once the taxman has been paid!

9

Other financial matters

Value added tax (VAT)

The current level of income at which you need to register for and to charge VAT is around £58,000 p.a. This level is not likely to be reached if you are just starting up your own coaching practice unless you are in partnership with others.

Considerable extra work is involved in keeping VAT records and if you are obliged to charge VAT for your services at 17.5% this means you either have to put your fees up, which can result in fewer clients, or you lose a proportion of your income in VAT.

Sometimes it is possible to reduce income to stay below the VATable level. For example, if you are travelling for your business on behalf of a client and if the client pays for your rail ticket and hotel expenses directly then you do not need to claim expenses, which will then not appear as income. This has no effect on your taxable profits.

Bad debts

Bad debts are more likely to arise when people pay by invoice rather than cash or cheque at the end of each session. If you are invoicing monthly, covering say four sessions at £50 per session, then £200 can be painful to lose. Failure to pay after a single session can be more readily contained with the opportunity for discussion and, if necessary, amendment to the coach/client contract. In theory, of course, there is the small claims court which, as part of the local county court, is fairly easy to find, and where you can obtain a claim form. The Small Claims Court produces an excellent booklet on how to use its services and the staff are always willing to offer advice.

There could still be the problem of enforcing the court's judgement in what is a civil rather than criminal case. You may not wish to employ bailiffs to hound a non-paying client or to spend an undue amount of effort debt-chasing.

When dealing with organisations you have little choice but to invoice them since you have probably agreed to do this as part of your contract with them. You may experience delays in being paid and you may need to remind them but they are less likely to want to suffer the embarrassment of court action.

The government has, somewhat belatedly, recognised the weaker bargaining position of the small company or trader and introduced legislation to curb late payers. Penalty interest of base rate plus 8% is payable but, again, you may not wish to alienate the customer.

Keeping receipts

It is easy to forget to obtain or keep receipts, especially for relatively minor cash items such as postage, stationery, taxi fares etc., but they all add up. If you do not have a receipt for an item you cannot claim it as a tax-deductible item. The simplest method for keeping receipts is to keep them all in chronological order clipped together in a cash tin and at the end of the month staple them all together and place in a brown envelope, clearly marked on the outside with the month and year.

Insurance

One of the last things on your mind needs to be one of the first things you think of when you start in business on your own. If you have previously been employed, then you may well have taken for granted the insurance coverage that your employer provided for you: if you were sick, you still got paid; if your office equipment was stolen, someone would replace it for you; and if you had an accident on company property, it was taken care of.

Now you will need to think about providing this type of insurance cover yourself. You may decide to take out insurance for the following reasons:

- To protect yourself from something happening to your income.
- To protect yourself from something happening to your health.
- To protect yourself from something happening to your belongings.
- To protect yourself from being sued by a client for an accident on your property or for (what they see as) their taking advice from you that led them into difficulties.

It is important to take the time to think about your own particular insurance needs. Insurance is expensive, and while on the one hand you want to be fully protected from disaster, on the other hand you don't want to pay high premiums that are hard to afford to be covered for things that are unlikely to happen. So take a moment to think about the following.

What if my home or office burns down?

If you are planning to work from home, it may be that your buildings and contents insurance will already cover you. It is also important to remember that you need to check with your insurance company to see whether running your practice from home affects your contents policy. Some insurers will not cover you when you run a business from home, while others will place a waiver on the policy. Such a waiver may state that the policy will only pay out if it can be proved that there has been forced entry. This kind of waiver is meant to avoid providing cover when clients leave your premises with your goods after they visit. There are now a number of insurers who provide specialist home-worker policies and it is worth investigating these.

If you are practising from rental premises you should also check what insurance is actually carried by the landlord; it may be only accidental damage to the premises themselves. It almost certainly won't cover any contents belonging to you and may not cover injury to third parties.

What if I find that all my office equipment has been stolen?

You will need to make the same checks on building and contents policies as for your premises, above.

What if I could not work for an extended period of time, due to ill health or accident?

Illness or injury to a self-employed person can have a devastating effect. No income is received but many personal and business expenses are still incurred. A few days are manageable but a few months could ruin your business, and what happens to your clients? When this happens, the differences between being employed and being self-employed can be appreciated – painfully. There is no six months on full pay and six months on half pay or whatever employment conditions prevail. You will find yourself in financial difficulties, and the worry of losing your business can add to your problems and perhaps lead you to return before you are fully recovered.

The downside of this type of health insurance cover can be the cost of contributions. It may prove more economical to keep a minimum of three months' money in a building society, earning interest, to be called upon should you be unable to work. Most bouts of illness that are likely to keep you from working are probably going to last between one and six weeks, and therefore a reserve fund of 12 weeks should be more than enough to provide the financial cover you will require.

What would happen if a client has an accident on my premises?

There is indemnity insurance against professional negligence or malpractice. It is important that all private practitioners have suitable professional indemnity cover. Defending oneself, even if the case is found in favour of the practitioner, is a costly business which causes a considerable amount of emotional distress.

What if I make some sort of professional mistake and a client sues me?

Again, indemnity insurance should cover this.

Thus, a number of insurances may be applicable:

- Building and contents
- Public liability (accidents to third parties on your premises)
- Professional indemnity
- Illness/loss of earnings.

For insurance advice, use an insurance broker. A broker is a professional salesperson who earns a living from commissions from the companies whose policies s/he sells. S/he may represent one company (i.e. is an exclusive agent) or a variety of companies (i.c. is an independent agent). Do not be afraid to shop around to get the best quotes. It is extremely important to use someone in whom you have trust and confidence, so that you feel comfortable that you are receiving good and honest advice.

Retirement planning

Just as you plan your career, so it is beneficial to plan your retirement, which these days can last as long as or longer than your career itself, particularly with early retirement at, say, 50 or so.

In planning for retirement, there are two main considerations:

- Will you have enough money to live comfortably and do the things you want to?
- What will you do with your permanent holiday?

An enormous amount of newsprint is devoted, particularly in the weekend papers (when they think, quite rightly, that we have more time to study such things), to all aspects of pension planning, personal investments, pitfalls, tax breaks, annuities, PEPS, ISAs and the like. This book is not the place to list every possible consideration or to make financial recommendations.

However, for genuine independent advice, we would recommend *The Which Guide to an Active Retirement*, which covers virtually every topic relevant to retirement and planning for retirement. There is a new edition every year or so to keep up to date with the latest government legislation, regulations and schemes.

The best time to start making provision for retirement is now (if you have not already started). The reason for this is the compounding effect of interest (or re-investment of dividends or returns), which can generate a large sum over a long period. For example, you could invest £3,000 in a cash ISA currently yielding 4.75% tax free. If it were possible to leave this investment for years at the same tax-free rate of interest then it would grow as follows:

- After 10 years £3,000 would turn into £4,731.
- After 20 years £3,000 would turn into £7,462.
- After 30 years £3,000 would turn into £11,767.
- After 40 years £3,000 would turn into £18,559.

Of course, if it were possible to invest £3,000 every year under the same conditions the final sums would be much larger – £193,353 after 30 years and £343,121 after 40 years – still significant sums of money and all yours! There would be no obligation to buy an annuity, although you could construct your own by living off the interest and prudent amounts of capital. There would be no charges by pension-providing companies to pay their administrative costs and shareholders either!

We are not necessarily recommending the above approach but a real and virtually risk-free return of 2.75% is good, historically (4.75% less 2% inflation). The point of the above example is to illustrate the impact that regular savings can make over a long time.

Providing for a pension does not necessarily mean signing up to an "approved" pension scheme or pension provider. However, the advantages of using a Treasury (or Inland Revenue) approved pension provider or scheme are:

- You get tax relief (up to certain limits) on your contributions.
- You don't have to do any work regarding investment choices.
- The pension provider may (but not necessarily) know more about investments than you do.

The disadvantages are:

- With few exceptions, you cannot deal directly with the pension provider and if you do you still pay commission. You are obliged to use an agent who will take a generous commission – possibly the first year or so of your contributions. This is done, strangely, with the permission of the pension providers themselves, who have threatened insurance brokers who wish to return a proportion of their commission to the customers with no business!
- Apart from the commission payable, there are administrative charges every year that are not always declared up-front to the customer.
- The current Chancellor of the Exchequer, in one of his renowned stealth taxes, has removed the tax-exempt status of pension investments in equities (stocks and shares) by pension providers, thereby cutting the return payable to their customers.
- Of the fund built up on your behalf, no more than 25% can be taken as a tax-free lump sum on retirement (without going into the business of draw-down arrangements). The rest must be taken as an annuity (typically 7–8% of the fund value at normal retirement age). When you die, any residual amount in the fund becomes the property of the pension provider.

Pension provision for self-employed people

A significant advantage to being employed by a company with a staff superannuation scheme is that the employer also makes contributions to your pension fund.

There is a range of options and possibilities for self-employed people:

- This may seem strange but at the present time one of the best options is to repay capital off your mortgage, if you have one. Since tax relief is no longer available and special offers of discounted mortgage rates have a relatively short life, you are likely to save more than if you invest in a cash ISA – typically about a 1% advantage.

time to pay your state pension. With a rapidly growing ageing population, the taxation burden on earners and companies to fund an acceptable level of state pension would become intolerable – hence the various tax breaks and concessions to encourage pensions and saving and reduce dependence on the modest state provision. Some countries do it differently, loading extra costs on employers (e.g. France, Germany) to subsidise higher state pensions, but this then reduces their competitiveness, which is one reason why there is pressure on EU governments for taxation harmonisation.

With state provision at a low level and likely to remain so, your own savings for the future will probably determine your standard of living on retirement. The earlier you start to put money aside the better, and it is sensible to take advantage of any tax concessions available.

As a test, sit down now and work out what your income is likely to be in retirement, preferably in real terms, i.e. after inflation. Will you still have a mortgage or other commitments to meet? You will probably need an income of at least half of what you are getting at present to maintain a reasonable standard of living. Do the sums and take action now. Make arrangements for standing orders at your bank so that you don't see the money you are saving and are not tempted to spend it. When you get more income, increase your standing order accordingly.

Other retirement considerations

People who have been used to a daily routine of paid work can find retirement unsettling. Whereas before weekends and holidays were to be treasured, looked forward to and enjoyed, suddenly all days become the same. Every day is a holiday. How can that feel when the days turn into weeks, months and years? Some lose a sense of purpose, direction and status, not realising how their daily contacts with others at work gave them a sense of fulfilment or achievement. Ordinary work pressures – to turn up on time, look presentable, behave properly, organise oneself and one's work, perhaps please a boss and get praise – disappear.

For many people, the work ethic has become a powerful learned habit and, without it, they don't know what to do.

In a number of ways, self-employed people are better able to cope with retirement since their work discipline comes from within rather than being externally imposed by an employer. You have the choice of working 20, 40 or 60 hours in a week, or even none at all. You can, up to a point, vary the type of work you do – one-to-one coaching can give way to training or writing. You can restrict yourself to certain types, or numbers, of client. If you have the money, you can take extended leave or holiday. You can attend courses to develop your knowledge or skills in areas of interest.

Nonetheless, it is an unusual person who wants to work until disability, illness or death dictate otherwise.

As mentioned previously, it is possible to draw a pension from your own pension fund from the age of 50. Of course, the benefits of retirement at 50 would be far fewer than retirement at 60, 65 or later, since the fund has to cover you for more years, possibly 30 or 50 rather than 15 or 20. Even so, it is an option, particularly if you have made substantial pension provision or savings beforehand. Perhaps the mortgage has been paid off and children are self-supporting, so financial commitments are much reduced.

It is not an objective of this book to tell you what to do when you retire. This is very much a matter of personal preference. However, it is important to give it some thought and planning. Retirement can be broken down into four aspects – the four Fs:

Finances	(what most of this section has been about)
Family and friends	(the opportunity to strengthen relationships)
Fitness	(to maximise your retirement years)

Reflection issues

- Have you given any thought to pension planning?
- If you are leaving employment for self-employment, have you considered the options with regard to the pension you have already built up?
- Does the realisation that you will no longer have an employer to contribute to your pension concern you? To what extent?

Having read this section, what issues in it do you believe that you need to address?

How will you do this?

Issue	Action	By when?	Done?

By tackling these issues, what results have you achieved?

If you have been unable to tackle any of the issues you have listed, what has prevented you?

What do you need to do to rectify the situation?

PART 4

Selling your services

10

Marketing

Marketing is a means of developing your client base. It means assessing the needs of potential clients and responding to them. It means letting as many people as possible know not only what you do but also how good you are at it. It means encouraging them to want to purchase your services. It is an on-going task. At the start-up of your practice, it may occupy a lot more of your time than actual coaching, and you will always spend a good part of your working week on it. However brilliant you are as a coach, you still need clients if you are to run a successful business, and they are unlikely simply to knock on your door, or call in while passing by. One coach (Martin, 2001) suggests that you should allocate at least 40% of your time to marketing.

Targeting your market

Also called market positioning, this is a vital first step in your marketing strategy. You will be a more successful coach if, instead of trying to be all things to all people, you make an informed decision about the type of clients you are best suited to work with. Only once you have decided that, should you start to look at where these identified client types will come from.

Your market profile will depend on how you commence your practice – whether you start in a small way, while still holding down another full- or part-time job and working on a shoestring budget, or whether you "go the whole hog" and start full-time, devoting all your energies and a large budget to your business.

With limited resources, you should aim your marketing towards individual clients, at least to start with. Your marketing expenses will be fairly low – perhaps a home-designed and home-made brochure and a small amount of local advertising will be enough to secure your first clients.

If you intend to aim at the corporate market, then you will have to make a much larger investment of time and money. You will face competition from major consulting firms, management training companies, business strategy organisations, well-known consultants and even legal and accounting firms that see coaching as a useful adjunct to their list of services. Therefore, you will need professionally designed and printed marketing materials, stationery and business cards of a very high quality so that you will catch the eye of the decision-makers whose business you are competing for. Your whole outlook will have to be one of the highest standard of professionalism. Your competitors have millions of pounds to spend on marketing and advertising. They have professional sales teams simply to bring the business in, after which the consultants take over and do the actual coaching work. You have to be all these things – marketing person, sales person and coach, and you have to do them all very well. It may take you a long while to secure a contract, and a lot longer to get paid at the end of it. It can be hard to break into the corporate market without knowing the right person, through networking or a personal referral.

On the other side of the coin, the upper level of fees that you can charge private clients is going to be much lower than those that a large company will pay. Corporate business is unquestionably much more lucrative, so even if you start up slowly, it may eventually be your aim to break into this market as your practice builds. And once you are known to a company, the chances are that they will use your services on an on-going basis – that is, they will act as "client finders" for you, whereas an individual client will only work with you for a limited period and then you will need to look for a replacement.

Here are some points to consider when defining your target market:

- How much time and energy can you give to marketing?
- How much money do you have available to invest in professionalising your marketing?
- Enthusiasm is vital. You will only be able to generate real (and

contagious) passion and energy if you are truly interested in the market you are targeting. Without these qualities shining through, you will be unlikely to convince people to purchase your services.

- What is your background? Will you relate more to people with business problems because you have spent many years working in business yourself? What are your personal strengths and weaknesses? You will find it much easier to attract clients with whom you have something in common.
- Age is important. It is unlikely that a 58-year-old CEO will listen seriously to a 25-year-old with limited experience, no matter what qualifications you have. So target an age range that avoids this sort of discrepancy.
- Geography matters! While one of the nice things about coaching is that it is very portable, and you can do it "any time, any place", you are still most likely to find the majority of your clients within a certain geographical radius of your home. Even though you may argue, "I am specialising in telephone coaching, so geography is irrelevant", actually, it *is* still relevant. You will become known in your area. You are more likely to be able to network regularly in your area. Local advertising will fit your budget, whereas national advertising will break your budget. For corporate coaching, you will possibly have to visit a company many times over before you "clinch a deal", and this type of regular contact is not easy if the company is far away from your own location. Even telephone costs for clients calling you will be a consideration (for them), and so will the bonding between coach and client that comes from the fact that they know the same areas and landmarks. All this is more powerful than you might think. The bottom line, therefore, is that a high-density locality will yield more clients for you than one of low density.
- Avoid over-generalising. Do not try to appeal to everyone around, and do not target too many different markets at once. Specialise somewhat, and you will be able to offer just that little bit more specific expertise than the next coach. You will also have a better focus on the markets you are appealing to.
- Review your marketing successes. If you are targeting areas which have given you a very poor positive response over a long period of time, consign them to the bin and look for

a new, possibly more productive market to replace them. Spend some time analysing why this particular market did not produce work, so that you can avoid making a similar misjudgement next time.

Please consider all of the above very carefully. Whether you are starting your practice up full-time or part-time, you will still only have a limited amount of time, financial resources and energy. If you squander these by targeting markets that are not very likely to produce purchasers of your services, your business may come to a grinding halt. Remember, the "product" you are selling is non-standard and made to order (rather than standard and supplied from stock) and this sort of business is always more difficult to manage since different blends of skills are required in each case, which are not necessarily obvious from an initial assessment.

In summary, what market you target is personal to your own wishes and desires. But it is wise to take into account what you have been trained to do, what you are good at doing, what your preferences are and what the needs or desires of the potential clients in your catchment area are. You can extend your product range through further training but your productive capacity is limited by the number of client contact hours you can manage in a week. Use these hours to maximum effect.

Having defined your market, you will need to consider the different possible vehicles for marketing your business, and we shall look at these now. They range from "hard sell" (such as advertising) to "soft sell" (perhaps speaking engagements) and others in between (the internet, for instance), and even marketing yourself – do you project the right image for the potential clients you are appealing to?

Let's look first at . . .

Traditional advertising

Certain businesses benefit from advertising, while others do not. Is coaching a business that would benefit? You could start by asking yourself the question, "If I saw an advertisement for my services, would it attract my attention?" Some coaches are quite dismissive of the value of advertising. Fairley and Stout (2004,

p. 128) say: "[T]he only time I can really recommend using traditional advertising is after you have tried everything else, it hasn't worked, and you still have a lot of money left over that you cannot think of anything better to do with." However, this is a personal view, and we feel that it is worth looking at the different types of traditional advertising you might consider, as one or two may especially appeal to you.

Do remember that advertising is an expensive route to finding clients, compared to others that we shall discuss shortly. How much money, if any, you have allowed in your budget for this will dictate the type that you purchase.

Yellow Pages

This is probably the best form of advertising if you are budgeting for any at all. This is one place people will often go to if they want a service that they cannot find by any other means. The disadvantage is that a *Yellow Pages* advertisement is not going to catch anyone's eye. The person must already have made the decision to look for a coach before s/he turns to that section in the directory. So in this case, you are not encouraging someone to seek coaching, but rather to choose you from the various coaches (if there are any others) advertising their services under the same banner.

What is going to make a client more likely to choose you? Well, there are certain things that are outside your control such as your geographical location, but there are also one or two things that are within your control.

- For example, where you are competing with several other similar advertisements, paying a little extra to have yours "boxed", or for a little extra lineage to explain your service in more detail, can be very worthwhile. It can also give people a feeling of confidence in you – "S/he must be good to have bothered with a professional style of advertisement."
- Another helpful "ruse", for want of a better word, is to try and start your company name with a word that begins with an early alphabet letter. For example, Axis Coaching Associates will get a listing far ahead of Whiteside Consulting. You will be surprised how many people simply telephone the

first name that they see, and work on through the list alphabetically.

Be sure that you choose the *Yellow Pages* most local to you, and stick to just that one to start with while you test the market. You will be charged more for each extra directory you go into, and our experience has shown us that even when you are offering to coach over the telephone, people generally plump for whoever seems to work in their own locality.

Classified advertising

These are the "small ads" that you see in newspapers and journals. The problem here is that the costs are quite high, based on the fact that a very wide audience will see your advertisement. However, if you bear in mind that it is possible that not one of the people who read your advertisement has any interest in, or need of, coaching, it is quite possible that you have totally wasted your money. Again, ask yourself the question, "If I was looking for a coach, would I be looking in the classifieds?"

One possible exception to this might be during the pre-Christmas period. Newspapers and periodicals run pages devoted to Christmas gifts, which can be attractive to those of us who have not the faintest idea what to give various friends and relatives who already appear to have everything. They do have very high readership levels. It might be worthwhile to take an advertisement on this type of page, in order to suggest purchasing a coaching session for someone as a Christmas gift – perhaps explaining how coaching will help them to "Develop and stick to some excellent New Year Resolutions," for example. You might even want to add a "two for the price of one" offer. If you can make it sound attractive, it certainly would be a most unusual Christmas gift. And some readers may also decide to purchase this "gift" for themselves!

National magazines

Much as we would all like to see our names in print in established, glossy, specialist magazines, the cost – many thousands of pounds – would be completely prohibitive, and you still could not guarantee generating any business from this. Leave this form of advertising to the large multi-nationals with the mega-budgets.

Radio and television

You will be best served to use this route not for direct advertising (which will be very expensive) but to generate some PR by offering to go on and talk about your work. If you present yourself as an interesting guest or authoritative expert in this new and exciting field, radio stations may well be interested in offering you a slot to fill their airtime. This will give you added exposure, as well as the cachet – which you can use in your promotional literature – of being featured "on air".

Assuming you are confident in your coaching abilities, we suggest that you could offer to speak about coaching on behalf of your professional body. Discuss this with your media representative, who probably receives regular enquiries from the media.

Of course you could advertise as well if you wish to. However, broadcast media can be very expensive, and you may have very little control over presentation.

Direct mail

This can work, but again it may be a large outlay for little return. You have to have a great many fliers or brochures printed and delivered, either through the post or by hand, and the cost of this might be prohibitive. On the plus side, there are many organisations that will sell you a mailing list specific to your needs – for example, companies within a 30-mile radius, within specific industries, with a certain number of employees etc. – which will enable you to target your marketing far more specifically and may be of more help to you in generating leads.

Bear in mind, too, that you could purchase a list such as just described, and actually make direct personal contact with these organisations, rather than simply sending them a brochure.

The above are examples of what we call traditional advertising, and while you should consider them, we do not advise, at least until your business is well established and you can rely on a good, regular income, that you throw too much money their way. The likelihood is that the return on your investment will not be good.

General publicity

A way to get some general publicity for coaching – with the idea that if you trigger people's interest in the topic, some may want to take it further and actually book a coaching session – is to offer to write articles on coaching for newspapers and journals. These will be welcomed, provided that the paper or magazine concerned does not feel that you are simply using it to generate free advertising. They are, quite rightly, fairly touchy about this. Therefore, to get an article accepted, bear in mind the following:

- The article should not be about you. It should be a general perspective on coaching, and not full of personal references.
- It should be written impartially. Don't wax too lyrical about the life-changing potential of coaching or, again, this may be seen as biased writing for personal gain.
- Offer to write on a specific aspect of coaching, with the suggestion that you would be pleased to write a series of linked articles on a regular or occasional basis if the paper would like this. This may lead to an opportunity to write regularly for the publication concerned.
- You must not try and "plug" your own practice in any way. Sometimes, newspapers will offer you the opportunity to place your details and telephone number at the end of the article, but leave this to them – don't insist, or you will appear too keen on self-promotion which will go against you.

Keep in mind that the goal of this sort of publicity is not especially to promote yourself. It is to get coaching in general into the public eye. The more people read about it, the more they will think about it, and perhaps see it as something they might like to try (which could be when your *Yellow Pages* advertisement comes into its own).

Positive publicity of this sort generates a general increase in the demand for coaching, which can influence the demand for individual practitioners. Make it part of your overall marketing plan to keep in touch with the editors of publications you work with, or hope to work with. Encourage them to regard you as an expert resource – journalists rely on quotes and information from experts to bring their own articles to life, and they will be happy to quote what you have to say if it is relevant.

Professional listing

Many people looking for a coach and uncertain where to find one may check with one of the several coaching directories that are available on the internet. It is therefore worth looking into having your own name or practice listed. While such directories are not yet especially in the public eye, it is possible that in the future they may become a standard resource for coaching enquiries. One or two suggestions are:

- Directory of Life and Career Coaches:
  http://www.quintcareers.com
- Classified Directory of Coaches and Business Coaches:
  http://www.banbury-cross.co.uk
- On-line Directory: http://www.associationforcoaching.com

Networking

We have just looked at the idea of general publicity for promoting coaching. Networking is a way of providing personal publicity for *you*.

Developing good networking skills is essential if you are to maintain a flourishing practice. Think of any sales or marketing professional you may know, no matter what their industry. Don't they seem to spend a great deal of their time at business lunches and dinners, wining and dining their clients in order to create opportunities subtly to promote their products and services? You will not be promoting your coaching business in quite this way, but it illustrates the fact that there is a direct relationship between the quality and quantity of your networking contacts and your sales figures. Martin (2001) suggests that you should be thinking in terms of using around 40% of your overall marketing time in making contacts.

Networking is important for a variety of reasons.

- Most importantly, it helps you to get yourself known to others, both individuals and organisations, which may lead to referrals.
- Regular attendance at relevant courses ensures that you keep your skills up-to-date, and gives you the opportunity to talk with the other coaches and consultants who attend.
- It gives you an opportunity to offer help to others where you have specific experience of, or information about, a problem they are dealing with. This cements relationships which again, in due course, may lead to referrals or other types of co-productivity.
- It prevents you from becoming too isolated, especially if you plan for networking events ahead of time, and space them out sensibly.

It is extremely important to plan your networking strategy carefully.

- You need to be pro-active. This means adopting a forward-looking view and actually seeking out and planning your networking activities. Do not simply rely on your "natural" networks of family, friends, old business associates, fellow golf club members or whatever. Actively seek new opportunities.
- Make your own network planner for the year ahead. Divide your planner into months, filling in the details of courses and events you plan to go to, and then see where the gaps lie. Work out how much time you feel you can give to networking on a monthly basis.
- Do not spread yourself too thinly! There is no possible way that you can follow up on every single prospect from a huge number of networking events. You will become confused and disorientated trying to follow up leads from hundreds of people or organisations you can hardly remember. You will put yourself under great stress and possibly do your business harm rather than good by presenting yourself badly. Quality will be far more helpful to you than quantity.
- Be selective about where you network. Networking takes time and energy and if you spend too much networking in the wrong places, you will exhaust yourself without any positive

results. Attempt to vary the type of networking that you undertake, and keep a written record of outcomes. Ruthlessly cut from your list anything that turned out to be a waste of time – no matter how socially enjoyable it was.

Networking opportunities take a variety of forms, and you will already be familiar with most of them. As you assess them, remember that there are only two good reasons for networking – for your own professional development and/or as a way of gaining possible new clients. Keep these two essentials in mind as you decide what to do and where to go.

Consider attending courses, conferences, workshops and events run by professional coaching bodies. Join any local trade or business associations and attend their functions and presentations. Offer to speak at one of these events and look for any other relevant groups you could offer to talk to. There is usually a variety of local groups and organisations looking for someone who can give an interesting talk to their members on almost anything. You may not be reaching your primary targets this way, but you can hope that those listening may be interested enough to tell other people, and that some of those they speak to may have more of a direct interest in coaching.

Make a list of local networking opportunities and try to add to this when you can. Register those that seem especially promising, and devote the majority of your efforts to them.

Even so, don't overdo this. It is quite possible to generate good leads through other methods, targeted "cold calling" for example, so ensure that your approach to gaining clients is a good mix of different styles and approaches.

The internet

Do you already have an internet website for your business? If you do, then that is good news for your coaching business. If you don't have one, have you thought about it? If not, why not? The internet is here to stay and your business will falter if you are not fully engaged with the facilities it offers. You will need to have a website if you are to appear up-to-date and professional, quite apart from the practical point that it will hopefully increase your client base.

We give you below a synopsis of the main considerations in setting up a website (we are going to assume that you already use email on a regular basis). These are:

- Registering a website name
- Designing your site
- The content of your site
- Maintaining your site.

Registering a website (domain) name

Your domain name is the name people will type into their internet browser to get onto your website. Registering a domain is very easy. Simply go to one of the hundreds of sites that register domain names, and it will tell you what to do. If you do not know of any, simply go to a search engine and type in the words "register domain name". You will get hundreds of choices! Otherwise see our appendix for a number of internet providers. You will of course be asked what you wish to call your website, and hopefully you will use common sense to avoid the pitfalls of choosing too long a name, a name that is easy to misspell or a name that gives no clue as to your type of business.

Do not forget that you will also need to choose a company to host your website, which means loading your website files on to a server connected to the internet, so that when people type in your website name, they will automatically be connected to your site.

Designing your website

Depending on your computer skills, you may wish to do this yourself or pay someone to do it for you. Your text will need to be translated into a format that an internet browser can read, and we are going to assume that not too many of you will have a good enough knowledge of the HTML codes to do this yourself. If you do not wish to go to the expense of paying a professional, there is a variety of software programmes with titles along the lines of "Build your own website" which are not especially difficult to master, as long as you can already use Microsoft Word or PowerPoint.

Some internet providers such as Bizland have free easy-to-use website templates. Even complete beginners can very quickly learn how to design their own websites. It can also be fun too.

If you decide to use a professional designer, you can either use someone local who is known to you, or find one on the internet. The second option will be cheaper, but you will be less confident of the quality of the designing. Because the standard of your website will reflect the quality of your business, we suggest that you pay for the best professional design that your budget will run to. It may be that potential clients will contact you about your services based solely on what they have read on your website. It therefore needs to reflect the highest professional standards and promote your best possible image.

Do not overload your website with photos, graphics, logos etc., for the simple reason that it takes about ten times as long to download graphics as it does to download text. Someone clicking on to your web page will lose interest within a few seconds if s/he is waiting for photographs and other graphics to download whose only purpose is to enhance the design. Terrific though it may all look once downloaded, your potential client may have moved on long before this is achieved. However, within the next couple of years the majority of surfers will be on broadband and no noticeable delay will be observed when downloading photos and large documents.

The content of your website

This is a part of the process that you will be able to undertake almost entirely yourself. If writing does not come too easily to you, however, you may wish to ask a literary friend to assist you, or to at least look over your work once you have written it.

A good first step is – again, via a search engine – to look at the websites of other coaches and make notes on what they put in (and leave out). Make some value judgements: if you were looking for a coach, which site would appeal to you the most? Why? What features/content might you incorporate in your own site?

Your website will probably consist of several pages, and the most important of these by far is your home page – the first page to come up when someone arrives at your site. Many people will only read this page, so be sure that it contains all the key points that you wish people to know about your practice.

A short overview of coaching and how it can help people in general will be a good start, as some visitors will not be especially familiar with the concept. Beyond this, your text should be punchy, creative and inspiring. It should focus on the outcomes and results that people can expect from coaching and then move on to why you, particularly, should be the coach of their choice.

Think hard about your goals for your website. For example, do you want it to highlight the information you already have in your brochure about your practice, or do you want it to offer a wider range of topics, for example coaching tips, up-coming events etc.? In other words, you can include items of interest that might encourage people to see your site as a resource and return to the site again and again. Whatever goals you have for your website, set them down clearly and ensure that the content you develop meets those goals.

Keywords and meta tags sound a bit technical. However, to get a high rating on search engines you may need assistance from a more website-literate colleague or consultant. Bear in mind also that there are websites that can provide free help and are worth visiting. For example, Submit Express has a simple tool that will analyse your website at no cost. It provides tips on how to improve your website and checks your keywords, loading time, links and file sizes. All you need to do is visit Submit Express, type in your website address and click. Within seconds the information appears. Website:
http://www.submitexpress.com/analyzer/

Submit Express also provides a tool to help you submit your website to 40 search engines. Again this is free:
http://www.submitexpress.com/submit.html

How many links are being made from other websites to your website? Hopefully over a period of time this will increase, bringing more potential business to you. You can check on the number of incoming links at the following website:
http://www.submitexpress.com/linkpop/

And if you need help choosing the most effective keywords for your website, check out their popularity first, at:
http://www.submitexpress.com/keytracker.html

There are other free web services that you could use. We have highlighted Submit Express as we have found it very useful. However, Scrub The Web is another good free service, with a meta tag check: http://www.scrubtheweb.com/abs/meta-check.html and a meta tag builder: http://www.scrubtheweb.com/abs/builder.html

One last point. Do use user-friendly language. Using technical, "insider jargon" may impress other coaches who are just logging on to check you out, but it will simply confuse and dispirit potential clients looking for a clear description of coaching in general and your services in particular.

Maintaining your website

This is one area a lot of people forget! How many times have you visited a website to find that the material on it is totally (sometimes by years) out of date? It is frustrating and unprofessional, and will not bring you much new business or give you credibility.

- You need to ensure that the information you give is always up-to-date.
- You must "ring the changes" with regard to both content and lay-out from time to time, so that there is a freshness to your site.
- The site should continue to reflect, with clarity, who you are and what you do, especially if your work specialities change over time.
- If you wish to develop an email database (perhaps for your newsletter – see next section), then give people a reason to let you have their email addresses. Suggest, for example, that they register in order to receive your newsletter, to win a prize or even receive a free coaching session. Then ensure that you regularly update and keep accurate this mailing list database.

If you have enough technical knowledge, you may decide to undertake this maintenance yourself. If you have used a professional designer, the chances are that s/he will also offer a maintenance service for a reasonable fee. If all else fails, ask your local college if any student studying computing would be willing to perform this service for you in return for payment.

Disability access

Since October 2004 there has been a legal requirement to provide access to website content to people suffering from visual impairment. It is not enough just to "show willing" by offering to send out a large print version of the website pages through the post (and consider how costly this might be).

There are some websites that may not need this facility – for example, those with limited graphic design elements – but the best way to ensure that you are on the right side of the law is to ask the website development company you are using to explain the new accessibility requirements to you. You can choose to ignore this advice, of course, but if a disabled reader chose to take action against you, you would find yourself in difficulty.

If you take up this option, your website will not ordinarily look any different to the normal design you have chosen: it will simply have, built in, the ability to take on different display features to cater for varying visual disabilities. These can be controlled by an "Accessibility" button on screen, and will offer choices such as, for example, light enlarged text on a dark background or dark enlarged text on a light background.

To find out more about these regulations yourself, see: http://www.disability.gov.uk

Email newsletters

You probably receive a great many of these already! They are one of the fastest growing promotional tools used by companies with a product to sell. If you have ever ordered anything over the internet, you have no doubt found that the company you placed your order with now keeps you regularly updated with what is happening in their world, what new products they have out etc.

You can adapt this resource for your coaching business, and it will be very effective – but also a lot of hard work. Having decided how often you will send it out ("occasionally" might be the best response to this while you monitor how much work it involves!), you will need to develop an email address list (and maintain it – new people will come on, others will ask to be deleted etc.) and then write regular copy for the newsletter, which will always need to be "up to scratch" if you are to present yourself as a high quality professional.

However, if you can cope with this, it is an excellent tool for keeping in touch with clients and potential clients, whereby you can promote any new services you are offering and remind them of the powerful benefits of coaching by a variety of different means. As with your website, it needs to be user-friendly, and also you should ensure that it is not overly promotional – coaching information and tips that appeal generally, rather than simply in relation to your own business, will give you credibility and stature.

Lastly, do remember the privacy of your readers. Only contact them using bcc (blind carbon copy) so that no email addresses are revealed, other than yours and the individual you are writing to.

11

Image

Your personal and professional image is a hugely important factor in the success of your business. Even if the majority of your work is over the telephone, there are many factors that will either contribute to, or detract from, your reputation.

As soon as a person meets or talks to you, he/she will start assessing you. Within the first 60 seconds he/she will have made a subjective assessment of your business acumen, personal character traits, level of professionalism and, if relevant, your ability to fit into their corporate culture.

Image isn't only a general impression that you give out. It includes, more specifically:

- How you look
- How you speak
- The way you act
- The quality of your written marketing materials and presentations.

Let's look at each of these in a little more detail.

How you look

The most important point is to dress in such a way as to make your clients feel comfortable. Drake (2001) suggests that this means dressing at least as formally as – or even slightly more formally than – the client. Since your clients may vary from casually dressed individuals to be-suited corporate people, you may wish to vary your style of dress to complement different environments. Don't assume that certain clients will respond better to a casual image of jeans and T-shirt, for example, in the belief that you look down-to-earth and friendly. Your clients may simply see you as being sloppy and uncaring and, by default, possibly not such a good coach either. You must respond to the client, not expect them to respond to you. In simple terms, ensure that:

- Your clothes are clean and uncreased.
- Your shoes are also clean, and appropriate to your outfit.
- Your jewellery – if any – is simple and unobtrusive.
- Your hair is clean and neatly styled.
- Your perfume or after-shave is minimal – and you have remembered to apply deodorant.

We suggest that you consider the above presentation ideas, within reason, even when undertaking telephone coaching, as how you feel, and therefore come across, may well be influenced by how you are dressed. Additionally, you should incorporate your business dress standards into your daily routine, whether mixing with others or not, so that it becomes a natural, unconscious process – and you never quite know who may knock unexpectedly at your door!

How you sound

As a coach, your voice is your most important sales feature and your most valuable asset. This includes not only what you say, but also how you say it. If your business is primarily telephone coaching, then the value of good speech goes up even further, as you have no possible pleasing visual qualities to counter your grating tones.

It may be helpful to tape-record your voice – reading aloud from a book or journal, for example – and listen to what you hear. Ask family and friends to listen as well, and give you honest views. If you get negative feedback, consider whether the comments highlight things you can change yourself, or whether it might even be worth purchasing some speech therapy to even out imperfections.

Make a checklist of important points (such as those below) and tick off the ones you need to work on.

You should:

- Speak clearly, ensuring that words are pronounced distinctly.
- Use "normal" English – don't use clever technical phrases or speak down to people.
- Use a varying tone and sound enthusiastic.
- Be courteous and polite at all times.

You should not:

- Speak too fast, too loudly or too softly.
- Sound over-familiar towards your client.
- Use slang, or profanities, or make ethnic or religious comments.
- Interrupt, or finish the other person's sentence.

How you act

We are always impressed by people who arrive at appointments on time, are pleased to see us, can remember our last conversation, have a friendly but professional attitude, and can answer almost any relevant question either from memory or by an immediate reference to notes or books which are readily to hand. Such people convey an instant confidence that they know their business and have done their homework.

Non-verbal communication – how we stand, sit, fold our arms, cross our legs, make eye contact etc. – all counts either for us or against us. Maintaining an interested focus on the client, while at the same time not leaning too far into their space (or standing too far away from them so that they have trouble feeling connected to you) is obviously important. There are also obvious "no-nos", such as

- Not "fiddling"
- Not smoking
- Not looking out of the window as you speak
- Not moving too much (crossing and uncrossing legs, for example)
- Not chewing gum.

In a nutshell, don't do anything that might make the client feel uncomfortable, and keep your attitude and your demeanour positive and enthusiastic.

Your marketing materials

Your image is identified not only by your personal presentation, but also by your presentation materials: stationery, business cards, sales brochures etc. You could throw an unlimited amount of money at this, and we have already referred to the fact that some companies spend a large amount of money on what is called "corporate image". Your main considerations should be:

- What is my budget?
- What is my market?
- How good am I at computer design?

Your budget

Your budget may be quite small at first if you are taking the "safe" route and building up your business slowly while you test the market. If your resources are limited, you should decide whether you would like to:

- Give this money to a professional designer, who can supply you with a logo and stationery design that you can then use on your own computer.
- Do your own designing, and then spend your money on a print firm, who will be able to give you a more professional look with better quality card, possibly embossed printing etc.
- Go it alone entirely, and do all your own designing and printing to keep costs to a minimum.

In making this decision, do bear in mind that your professional image is very important. If you are planning to "cold call" companies with written information, then the standard of your stationery and brochure may make a real difference to pulling in clients. So do give all this serious consideration.

Your market

The potential market that you decide to target will also have a bearing on how much you decide to professionalise your written material. Where you are primarily targeting individuals, you may be wasting your money with an expensive brochure. In fact, it might even put some clients off as they will assume that your fees reflect the cost of this sort of expensive printing. However, if you are planning to move into corporate coaching, then – as we have mentioned before – you will be competing with a variety of coaching organisations, management consultancies etc., and your presentation needs to be of a competitive standard so that you do not look like a "poor relation". Thus, decisions about your target market will also have bearing on decisions about your presentation materials.

Your computer design skills

Your own computer and design skills will also be a factor. If you are familiar with desk-top publishing, enjoy designing and have a good quality printer, then you may well feel that you can produce something that will be just as good as a professional. This also means that you can tinker endlessly with your designs while you achieve the look that you want. One middle-of-the-road solution here is to find a designer on the internet who will create a design and download his/her design files to you. This means that you can continue to play with the design if you wish. This option is far more economical as far as your brochure is concerned, as you can simply print them up as you need them, rather than having boxes of them in the garage that become out of date before you have used them all.

The three main items of stationery that you need to consider are:

- Headed notepaper
- Business cards
- Brochure.

Headed notepaper

People have different ideas about the best image for notepaper, and if you are stuck for ideas you can ask a designer to submit three or four to you in basic form (i.e. let him/her know that you don't want to pay for detail until you have a feel for what you want). Do you want a logo? This is not necessary, but certainly will give a more professional look and feel to your business. It can also "soften" the wording on the page.

You will want to give time to ensuring that your company name is the one you want, and reflects the image you are looking to create. Do not automatically give the business your own name. Of course, this may be your genuine preference, but do also explore other possibly more creative and exciting options first. Avoid using the name of the town or city you work in as part of the title (e.g. "Coventry Coaching"). If your business does eventually expand, then you may limit yourself by suggesting that you only operate in a certain geographical area.

Once you have decided on your name and your logo, typeface is also important. There is an enormous choice of very fancy styles, but we suggest that you choose a typeface that is modern, simple and offers absolute clarity regarding lettering and numbers. We have received wonderful-looking letterheads but we have strained to read the wording and even been uncertain as to what it said, simply because the typeface chosen was so elaborate.

Most importantly, ensure that you include every possible way for a person to contact you on your stationery – apart from the obvious address and telephone number, email is now almost mandatory, your website, if you have one, is important to mention, and a fax (if you have one), mobile and/or pager number all need to be clearly shown.

If you are having your stationery professionally printed, it is a good idea to ask for some compliments slips as well.

Business cards

Fairley and Stout (2004) refer to business cards as the cheapest marketing tool ever created. This is absolutely right! You can never have too many, and you can never give too many out. So don't scrimp in this department.

The design of your card will probably follow the stationery design. The most important issues are the colour and quality of the card, and whether you decide to make them yourself on your computer or have them professionally printed. Our advice is: if you have just one thing professionally printed, then it should be your business cards. You will not make a good impression handing out flimsy, plain white cards – even worse where you can still see the perforation ridges! The most impressive cards will be printed on a card that is much thicker than you can run through your home or office inkjet printer. A coloured card is also more attractive than white, and an unusual finish to the card (e.g. a linen or vellum look) can add extra quality.

You should be able to get several hundred business cards printed for around £50 or so, and this is almost certainly a worthwhile expense.

Finally, once you have them, don't keep them in a drawer. Have them with you all the time, wherever you go, and hand them out liberally.

Brochure

Putting together your brochure will be a major time and energy consumer. It may – but does not necessarily need to – cost you a lot of money.

As mentioned already, you may wish to do this entirely yourself to start with, to keep costs to a minimum, or you may go for a slightly more costly solution and get an internet designer to do it for you and send the design to you as a download. You will be much better served by being able to print the brochure off at home, as you can regularly upgrade it as your business grows and changes.

When considering content, keep consistently in your mind the primary goal of your brochure. This should be to encourage the person reading it to pick up the phone and get more information on your services. You want your brochure, therefore, not to be just a list of your services or a personal biography of your background, but rather to:

- Give an overview of what coaching is, and its recent development.

- Suggest problems or challenges that clients might wish to overcome and how coaching could help them with these.
- Tell them what sort of results they can expect. This means promoting strongly the outcomes that they might achieve.
- Explain to them the benefits of achieving such objectives.

You want to convey not just what you offer, but how good what you offer actually is and what benefits there will be to the client. Back up your claims with evidence that coaching does work. You might wish to cite a CIPD (Chartered Institute of Personnel and Development) training and development survey, released in May 2004, which showed:

- 99% of the firms interviewed agreed that coaching could deliver tangible benefits to the organisation.
- 90% believed that coaching can positively influence the bottom line.
- 67% of respondents rate coaching as "very effective" or "effective".
- 49% said that finding high-quality coaches was a difficult task.

Source: CIPD, May 2004. See www.cipd.co.uk/training/cm

Do keep your messages short, punchy and to the point, with lots of bullet points. Most people will simply glance over your brochure rather than read it in detail, so you need to make quick and positive impact.

You do not need to spend a great deal of money on your corporate image. Simply make sure that it appeals to the market sector you are hoping to work with, that it has a professional feel to it, that it is attractive visually and clear and easy to read. If you do this, and make sure that your personal presentation is good, you will ensure that both current and potential clients get the best possible impression of both you and your business.

It is possible that you may wish to offer inducements in your brochure, such as a free coaching session: "If you are holding this brochure in your hand, then you are entitled to a free introductory coaching session which you can book by ringing the following number . . ." Whether you do this or not will depend on how widely you plan to circulate your brochure. If you plan

standing or influence, empathetic to the idea of coaching, and with whom you have a comfortable and mutually respectful relationship. Equally, they may be new connections – people you have met at a networking event with whom you have got on especially well, perhaps.

Take the time to make a written list of possible good referral sources, and constantly add to it and refine it.

How can I meet them?

As we have already mentioned, you will need to give time to attending various networking events. At such events you will come across certain companies and individuals where you feel that developing a closer relationship would be mutually beneficial. Remember that developing a coaching referral relationship can take some time, and you are looking at a long-term investment rather than some quick income (unless you are exceptionally lucky). So you will need to "track" them, in the sense of ensuring that you attend the same functions and events that they do, and that you get many opportunities to chat with them over a period of time.

How do I sell myself when I am with them?

The answer to this is, only in the "softest" way. We are tempted to say, "You don't", that not selling yourself is actually a way of selling yourself, and you will hopefully understand this. You will create these referral prospects, which you hope will be on-going, not by plugging yourself and your business but simply by learning about them and their business, and being interested in their successes and their problems. Have genuine curiosity and ask intelligent questions such as "How has your industry changed over the last decade?" and "What are your biggest challenges in the current climate?" and a variety of similar enquiries that you can tailor towards a company or an individual. Listen closely to the answers.

Developing this sort of rapport will usually be a two-way process. Sooner or later, you will be asked what you do, and you will have an opportunity to say something about coaching in general and your business in particular. As always, focus on the outcomes of coaching, not the tools of coaching. Don't find yourself giving any sort of sales pitch. An obvious question might be along the lines of "Do you ever use coaching in your company to develop individual performance?" or, for an individual, "Have you ever felt that having some professional support might help you to reach your personal goals more easily?" You are always simply looking to develop a coaching conversation, and interest your prospect in the idea of it. Never go beyond this to asking them if they would like to use your services. You are developing an enduring relationship at present, and that is your goal.

What can I do for them?

What can *I* do for them? Yes, actually, we do mean this! To cement this relationship, you need to consider how knowing you might be helpful to this person or his/her business. S/he also needs to consider this relationship as one worth developing. For example, you could suggest that you would be pleased to recommend their services to others, or to let them know if you come across organisations or individuals that would be good prospects for their own business. It may be that you know of a particularly good financial adviser/legal expert, for example, that you would be pleased to put them in contact with.

If you feel it is appropriate – probably where they have expressed some knowledge and understanding of coaching, or at least an interest in finding out more about what you do – you might offer them a free coaching session, "Simply so that you can see what it is like in action". Alternatively, though similarly, you might suggest offering one or two sessions to staff in the company your prospect owns or works for. This should be offered on an informal and friendly basis, rather than an obvious "foot in the door" approach.

How much time should I give to developing a referral network?

Quite simply, as much as you can. Developing referral prospects in this way is quite likely to be the best source of on-going clients that your business will ever have, and it is therefore worth giving planned time to it on a regular basis. As always, plan on paper, with a diary, and ensure you meet the networking targets that you set yourself.

13

Converting enquiries

If you have taken up some of the marketing ideas we have given you, and are devoting your time and energies to them, they should be starting to generate some enquiries. Some may be via letter or email, some may be face-to-face, but the majority are going to be over the telephone.

This telephone conversation is likely to be the most important one you will have in relation to converting an enquiry into a solid client. You must therefore make the most of this opportunity.

At the start of the conversation, it is extremely important to listen closely to what the potential client wants, rather than be too eager to tell him what you do. The more information you gather early by good listening, the more you will be able to tailor what you eventually say to the client to their exact needs, rather than taking a "one size fits all" approach. Your role at this stage is to ask intelligent questions of the enquirer, to establish exactly what they are hoping for from coaching.

Once you have clearly established whom you are talking to and what they are looking for, you can describe how the services you offer will fit very well with their needs. Again, don't simply tell the enquirer what you can offer – describe what you do in terms of a "good fit" with what they are looking for and what outcomes they can expect. This part of the conversation should take some time, as it is the heart of the enquiry.

Hopefully, by this stage you have an interested potential client on the other end of the telephone. This may be a good time to offer, for example, a free coaching session so that they can try your services out. It is actually quite hard for someone to resist something that is free. If you are less certain of the seriousness of the enquiry, you may alternatively prefer initially simply to offer to send your brochure, as a free session is quite a commitment on your part.

Strange though it may sound, you will be well served – where the potential client continues to show interest – by asking them whether they have any concerns about undertaking coaching, either for themselves or for their company. For example, "Can you think of any reservations you might have about using a coach?" The reason for doing this is that it gives you an opportunity to respond to any reservations they may have with convincing and positive arguments in favour of the benefits. You also have a chance to correct any misunder-standings they may have about the process.

If you don't do this, you risk the potential client putting the phone down and then considering all the downsides without you alongside to counter-balance or resolve them. In turn, this may mean the enquirer will decide against proceeding further – something you might have prevented had you been a little bolder.

You may already know some of the basic theories about making an impact when you give any sort of presentation or sales pitch. The most relevant to you with be those of *repetition* and *recency*.

First, keep in mind that people will only retain a certain amount of what you tell them. This is another good reason for not saying too much and making what you say succinct and to the point. While you are explaining the various services you offer, chances are that the person you are speaking to will be thinking something along the lines of: "I wonder how old this coach is? . . . He sounds as though he has a slight accent. . . . I'd better not let him go into too much detail before I find out what the fees are, in case this is a waste of time." These are, of course, slightly exaggerated examples of what are called parallel thought processes, where the person is listening to you with one ear but turning other things over in his/her mind at the same time, and thus not (necessarily) focussing entirely on your every word.

So you need to ensure, somehow, that the most important points you wish to make are, in fact, retained, and you can do this first by *repeating* them several times. Of course, we do not mean like a parrot, but integrating them intelligently into the conversation. Focus on referring back to the benefits and find subtle ways of reminding the enquirer of them on as many occasions as you reasonably can.

Second, use the concept of *recency*. We usually remember the last thing we hear far more easily than anything else. Why? Well, very often, simply because it was the last thing we heard! This is another good reason for asking that question about the enquirer's possible reservations earlier in the conversation. It means that you have got the negatives out of the way, and you can finish with a summary of all the benefits, thus ensuring that the positive aspects of your services are what the potential client remembers when he/she puts the phone down. If you have not "cleared" the reservations, the chances are, when you have finished your summary of benefits, that the enquirer may then express any concerns s/he may have, and this is what they will remember more prominently after the call is over.

Finally, you can end the conversation with the ball in your court if you so wish. "I have my diary here. Shall we set a date now for your coaching session/my visit to your offices?" or "Let me have your address and telephone number so that I can send you our brochure. I'll call you in a few days when you have had a chance to read through it." Always (of course) be extremely courteous when you end the conversation. Thank them for calling and for giving their time, and say that you hope to have the opportunity of speaking with them again. Even when it is obvious they are not going to take things further, your courtesy might encourage them to refer others to you in the future, or to return to you themselves at some stage.

It is worth noting that older established professional bodies in overlapping fields such as psychology may view initial free coaching sessions as an inducement and therefore poor practice and possibly unethical. As a Chartered Psychologist one of the authors of this book would not offer initial free sessions.

Summary

We hope that this section on the various aspects of marketing has given you a wide variety of options that you can tailor and personalise to your own business, and that we have also managed to emphasise the importance of it to your business. Create a marketing plan using the SMART model (Specific, Measurable, Achievable, Realistic and Time-limited) and then constantly review it and reshape it as your business grows and changes. With good marketing, you are giving yourself the best possible chance of success.

Reflection issues

- How can you feel more comfortable about selling your services?
- Can your new business survive without a marketing plan?
- Have you any possible contacts that may help you build up your referral network? How can you increase this network?
- Are offers of free coaching sessions good practice?

Having read this section, what issues in it do you believe that you need to address?

How will you do this?

Issue	Action	By when?	Done?

By tackling these issues, what results have you achieved?

If you have been unable to tackle any of the issues you have listed, what has prevented you?

What do you need to do to rectify the situation?

PART 5

Going into business

14

Creating the right environment

Starting out initially

The environment you select to work in is going to depend in part on how you decide to start up your business initially. Will you "go for broke" and immediately set up in full-time practice, or will you take a more cautious approach?

Up to now, we have made the assumption that you are a one-person business (i.e. a sole trader), and that you are working full-time. However, we are mindful that coaching is a career that offers the opportunity of full- or part-time work, which can take place not only during weekdays, but also in the evenings and at weekends. Therefore, we would like to take a look at all your various work options, in case there are some that you have not yet considered.

For example, you could continue with your present job, but start a part-time coaching practice in the evenings and weekends. This is the most financially secure way of starting your business, but you will need a lot of energy and, if you have a partner, they will need to be very understanding about the time involved!

A significant advantage is that you are testing the market – and your fee level – without undue risk. If clients are forthcoming and judge that your services represent good value for money, you will begin to build a reputation and enjoy client loyalty. It also gives you time to get your name in the relevant directories for advertisement purposes. If you reach the point in a fairly short space of time where you are turning clients away and referring them elsewhere, then you are either under-pricing your services or should considering moving to full-time self-employment.

Remember to consider your costs before becoming too excited by the extra income. It is gross rather than net. You may well have to advertise your services and equip a spare room, possibly installing an extra telephone line with an answerphone – and your extra income less business expenditure will be subject to tax.

For every upside, there is always a downside and, in this case, a big disadvantage is that you could be working up to an extra 10–12 hours per week on top of your day job. In a family situation, this will impact on any social or family life you may have enjoyed previously and probably affect your ability to carry out whatever share of household duties you were previously undertaking. An understanding partner and/or understanding children willing to give support is very desirable and you may well need to have considerable discussion and agreement before you start. Even if you are single, you will no doubt have a social life, use a gym, have hobbies and interests etc. – and only a limited amount of energy. A further alternative, therefore, might be to consider finding a part-time job that enables you to start coaching part-time during your non-employed days.

As before, this has the advantage of being relatively low risk financially and provides an opportunity to test the market and your own capabilities, with a little more flexibility and less chance of burnout than working full-time. You will need to give consideration to the working hours of the part-time job and whether they will fit in with freelance coaching work. For example, working in the evenings, if that is when your clients want to consult with you, will leave you with empty days free to no purpose. A part-time job where you might have the opportunity of flexible hours (home-working, for example) might be your preferred option if you seriously want to develop your coaching practice quite quickly. You may need to forego high pay in order to have this flexibility, but if you can balance your finances, it could be worth it.

Again, your overall income should improve since you have more paid hours in the week, but your income tax liability will also increase almost immediately since your personal allowance and the 10% tax band probably will have been used up in your part-time job. Nonetheless, such a situation represents a viable option.

Something else you could consider is joining an established coaching organisation that can offer you at least occasional regular work. In a sense, this is a similar option to the previous one, in that you are hoping to achieve at least some regular work that can assist with the outgoings, while you progress towards starting a full-time practice. Again, reducing the heavy costs normally associated with starting a new business from scratch may be very helpful to you. The disadvantage of pursuing this option is that there are only – at the time of writing – a handful of coaching organisations that would be likely to offer this type of work. So you would have to investigate the feasibility of finding this type of employment. It is possible that, if a coaching organisation itself has peaks and troughs, work-wise, it would welcome having someone to call on if needed. Your fees for this type of work are likely to be less than those you will gain from your own business, as the organisation you are working for is providing the clients and will, rightfully, take part of the fee for doing this.

Another way of reducing your initial overheads could be to set up a practice with another coach, or coaches. This might seem a very tempting option. After all, if doctors, dentists, lawyers and accountants can do it, why not coaches?

There are certain obvious advantages to working with other coaches:

- From a financial point of view, the rental and other costs associated with premises can be shared. It might even be possible to employ a receptionist/administrator/book-keeper to take the load off the coaches.
- It may be possible to provide mutual cover at times of illness and holiday.
- Where any one coach has an excessive number of clients, they can be referred to other members of the practice. However, it would be prudent to have a contract signed regarding how the practice would operate, including all the responsibilities of each coach.
- It may be that working with other coaches is a good choice until sufficient experience and confidence are acquired to go it alone.

The disadvantages, however, are numerous:

• The catchment area, particularly in sparsely populated rural regions, may provide only enough business for one individual. Even where you are offering telephone consultations, and geography is not quite so important, there may still be competition between you for a limited number of clients.
• You lose some of the individual control over the business and the way it is run. Problems may arise through differences of opinion and behaviour between the practice's coaches. There could be arguments over how income and expenditure are to be shared, whether all partners are pulling their weight, how the practice should or should not be developed and so on.
• From a legal point of view, the partners are generally all held to be responsible for all matters dealt with by the practice. Thus, malpractice of any type by one partner, if done in the name of the business, could involve all partners.
• Similarly, if one or more of the partners leave, then the remaining partners are responsible for all tax.

A good reason for considering the above options is that it can be difficult to launch straight into a full-time practice from scratch. You have to spend money setting the practice up and it takes time to expand your client base to a level which recovers your initial investment, your business expenses, pays you a reasonable personal allowance and allows you to provide for tax, business and personal development and a pension.

Of course, if you have ready-made referral sources in previously established contacts, then the time you need to give to publicising your services will be less, and you could probably start full-time from scratch. Otherwise, you do need sufficient capital to see you past the point of maximum cash outflow, as the section on financial planning will have shown you.

Which option you choose will depend on individual circumstances, the location of the practice, personal preferences and finances.

Premises

In all probability, the coaching services that you plan to offer will include both face-to-face and telephone coaching and, possibly, you will intend to look at the corporate market for clients, thus meaning that you will be working in a variety of locations. You will be unlikely, at least at the start, to limit your options by choosing only one market. Therefore you will be working from your own office at least part, if not all of the time, and will have clients visit you there.

You must therefore give serious consideration to where you will base your office/consulting room, and what will be involved in setting it up professionally for business.

There are two main options when it comes to the choice of premises for a consulting room: work from home or rent suitable premises.

There are a number of advantages and disadvantages associated with each.

Working from home

For someone starting in private practice, this has the significant advantage of low initial outlay. However, there are some unavoidable capital costs, and you need to consider the costs of furniture, equipment, carpets and curtains etc., and re-decoration.

Once your room is equipped, however, the day-to-day running costs will be marginal – little more than extra heating and lighting, telephone charges etc.

If the room is used exclusively for business purposes then there may be an additional charge in terms of business rates. This can be avoided if the room is also used for domestic purposes. However, if in doubt, check with your local authority for any regulations currently in force. Planning permission is not likely to be required unless the essential character of the house is changed (e.g. a large extension is built).

There are, however, some disadvantages. First, unless you have a large house or genuinely spare room which can be devoted to your business, it can be hard separating business from personal life. You will not appear very professional if your face-to-face clients accidentally bump into other family members on their way in or out, or telephone clients hear children shouting or a television blaring out in the background.

Second, pets can be a hazard. Unless you keep your coaching office door closed at all times, you may well usher a client who has a pet allergy into a room with a cat or dog snoozing on a chair. It can also be hard to disguise the smell of cooking, which can permeate a small household.

While people will no doubt be perfectly understanding about such incidents, it will detract hugely from the image of a completely professional service that you are wishing to create.

Nonetheless, when you are starting out this may be the only viable option. If this is the case, do plan ahead, and consider very seriously the issues we have raised here, and any others that are personal to you.

Renting premises

Generally speaking, renting suitable premises enables you to tailor-make a room as a professional consulting room. It may come ready furnished so, provided the furniture is suitable, you will not have to buy any. You will need plenty of desk space and storage for your telephone, computing equipment, books, files and stationery if you choose to do all your work from the office. Alternatively, you may decide to do all your paperwork at home and simply use the premises to see clients. The décor can be of your own choosing, together with curtains, floor coverings, pictures and so on. The working environment is more controllable by you and you don't need to worry about other members of the family or pets.

Of course, whichever premises are chosen, location, safety and convenience for clients are still important. You would probably not choose premises on an industrial estate. A residential or residential/retail environment is more appropriate, as used typically by doctors or dentists.

The main disadvantage of renting premises is the cost, which will vary according to location. You may have to agree a tenancy of 6 or 12 months and pay a month's rent as a deposit as well as paying the rent in advance. The landlord could decide to re-possess the premises (after giving due notice) or be reluctant to carry out necessary repairs.

In short, if you intend to take out a tenancy on business premises you should exercise the same care as you (hopefully) would for a residential letting, and some legal advice would be helpful to clarify your rights.

Another alternative is to rent premises only by the hour or day, in which case you are likely to be sharing the premises with others. This is generally a cheaper option than renting premises just by yourself but it restricts what you can keep in the office, and it also means that someone else is choosing the décor etc. However a further plus is that, in such an instance, the owner of the premises is probably paying all the necessary bills and taxes, and possibly also paying for contents insurance, cleaning, repairs, reception etc., so you know exactly what your commitments are – just the hourly or daily rate.

A variation on this option is a straight sharing of premises with one other person, either with a joint tenancy (where you are both liable for the rent, utilities bills, and council or business tax – and any damage) or with one of you being the tenant and sub-letting to the other. A landlord may be uneasy about this sort of arrangement as, with any agreement of this type, if one person leaves the landlord could be left with a potential squatter on his/her hands or a tenant who can't pay the rent.

Whichever option you choose, it is essential to know exactly what you are committing yourself to – and whether you are complying with local authority regulations and what legal liabilities you may be incurring, perhaps without realising.

Disabled access

Whether you are renting office space or using your own home, you must consider how you will offer disabled access, which will realistically mean that someone in a wheelchair can get from the street to your consulting room with relative ease. This means that you should not be considering a consulting room that is up a flight of stairs unless there is a lift or a ramp available. This may inhibit your choice of office location, but it is important to do so. If a client were to take action against you for disability discrimination, you would be in a difficult position. For fuller information on the requirements you must comply with, go to: http://www.disability.gov.uk

This excellent website will provide you with all the information you need to ensure that you are complying with all new disability laws. Do check it out – this is important.

The wider environment

Not only will you need to give consideration to the standard of your office, but also the rest of the premises as seen or used by your clients, and also the immediate neighbourhood. A client is likely to absorb the details of the environment, and possibly draw conclusions about the coach as a result. It is obviously important that these influences are positive rather than negative. A run-down environment could make a client feel somewhat nervous or threatened – or simply make the client wonder what sort of coach would choose such an environment to work in. Similarly, an unswept path or unkempt garden with litter will create an impression of a slovenly attitude or lack of care. Corridors, waiting area, toilets etc. do need to be kept clean, tidy, warm and attractive if you want the client to feel comfortable – and to return to your premises again.

Style of décor

The office and its furnishings may reflect your personal style, but you would be better served by adopting a very neutral approach to décor. If your idea of what is attractive is very different from that of some of your clients, then they will make judgements about you based on this, and will simply not feel comfortable in the environment you have created. It is also important not to have décor that is distracting to the client, as you will both want to concentrate on the session in hand. Keeping furnishings simple, and décor neutral, will facilitate this.

How do you feel about displaying your diplomas and accreditations? You will, understandably, be proud of your qualifications and may wish to display framed certificates on the wall. You may feel that, especially in an emerging profession such as coaching, it is important for clients to appreciate your professionalism and training. However, there are differing views about the display of such items. Some people do not believe that it is necessary to attempt to impress a client with such a display, believing that at the end of the day it is the application of knowledge and skills rather than their formal possession which counts. So this will be a personal choice for you to make. However, we recommend at least that these framed qualifications be subtly placed, rather than placed where they will hit the client in the eye.

Equipment needs

If you have sole or controlling use of your office, you can equip it as you see fit or are able to afford.

At a very basic level all that is needed are two, possibly three, comfortable chairs, window and floor coverings, space for storing client notes and details, a telephone answering machine and access to a toilet and wash basin.

However, the constraints of such spartan furnishing will soon make themselves felt. A desk with writing surface, a high chair, drawers for stationery and writing materials, and cupboards or bookshelves for files, books and publications would perhaps be the next priority.

Then might come décor, including appropriate lighting, pictures and perhaps a small table with a lamp. Finally, for an up-to-date working office, a personal computer, possibly with its own dedicated phone line, a printer, a scanner and a fax machine (preferably with its own line, though email may render this unnecessary). Lots more storage space is needed for the mature practice, particularly if the practitioner has diversified into writing or training. Training materials, professional journals and reference books can accumulate alarmingly.

There are many additions: facilities for tea or coffee making, storage of soft drinks, and more electronic equipment in the form of portable laptop, notebook or palm computers, and perhaps a zip drive for backing up files etc.

Consideration also needs to be given to peripheral space: a clean, warm and tidy toilet with paper, towels, soap and air freshener, an attractive entrance and passageway, clean and in good decorative order, and storage space for cleaning materials and equipment.

When you are initially starting your practice, this may all seem like far too large an outlay for an untried business, and of course you will make compromises to start with. However, do plan for the longer term. You can, for instance:

- Buy desks and units that can be added to in the future with other furniture of the same style, which will give a seamless, professional look.
- If you are getting a telephone line installed, enquire about the extra cost of having a second line put in at the same time. It is likely to be far cheaper than making this request at a later date.
- Think in terms of a secondary storage area – perhaps the attic if you are home-based and already using the spare bedroom, or the spare bedroom if you are using a downstairs study.
- If you are renting premises, ask if they have spare storage space – an archive room perhaps – that would be secure.

How you set priorities for the acquisition of office items, furniture, furnishings and equipment is obviously your personal choice. Cost, time saving and the creation of a pleasant environment may well be determining factors. Simply bear in mind that, as your business develops, you will be surprised how quickly you will need extra space and furniture, so do try to anticipate this.

Personal and client security

If you are working with face-to-face clients visiting your premises, we have already mentioned the need for them to feel they are in a comfortable and safe environment. Small details can help – an outside light for evening clients, keeping pathways swept and free from ice, cutting back on large shrubs that could hide a potential mugger etc.

Clients may also wish to keep their contact with you confidential, for a variety of reasons. If you schedule clients at intervals of an hour and a quarter this allows for a small over-run if necessary, as well as for the making of notes, preparation for the next session and avoidance of clients meeting each other. If you have a consulting room away from home and there are other people in the same building, think about the measures you need to take to ensure that your conversations are not overheard or disturbed.

When you leave your consulting room, make sure that no unauthorised people enter it, and that client notes and records are securely locked away. Depending on where you are working you might find it helpful to have a small, lockable, handheld metal filing system (freely available from main stationery stores) for current clients. Ex-clients could then be filed in a more traditional four-drawer lockable filing cabinet. If you are working from home you could store this cabinet in your garage. If you do, it is essential that it is locked and/or that the garage is suitably alarmed and/or locked.

Depending on how you obtain your clients – whether they are recommended to you or have simply answered an advertisement for your services – you do need to consider your personal security when you are with a client on your own.

On the assumption that when you work in your private practice – whether in an office or at home – you are often on your own, geographical location may be a first consideration. If your consulting room is very obviously a part of your home, the client may perceive it as linked to other rooms and there is no sense of isolation. Taking someone off to an annex might be a different issue.

Attempt to ensure that your coaching environment is light, bright and near to where other household members might be (even if there is no-one there). One strategy you can use is that of leaving a radio or television on in a room that you pass by on the way to the coaching room (having ensured that it is not audible once you are in there). This leads the client to assume that there are other people at home, and gives you more confidence in your security.

You also need to consider where your clients come from. Keeping the clients you are willing to work with face-to-face to those who are referred from reliable sources may also minimise any difficulties. You may decide to offer telephone coaching only to "cold call" clients who come to you without recommendation. You need to think about the difference between the acceptance of some inherent risk and an increase in risk factors that may shift the balance of safety.

Although we need to be aware of the slight possibility of aggression, we also need to recognise the rarity of such an event. Interestingly, we are most likely to encounter personal physical violence when we work in an office full of disparate colleagues!

Now let us just suppose that you are confronted by a client who seems to be becoming agitated in a way that suggests imminent violence in a session. What precautions can you take, and what can you do?

- Perhaps a little extreme, but it is possible to have a "panic button" installed in your office that is connected to your local police station.
- Where do you sit in your office? If you sit nearer the exit door than your client, this will give you an advantage if you need to leave the room quickly.
- Where you have the smallest doubt about a client in advance of a session, see if you might arrange for someone else to be around in the building. If you are really uncertain or uncomfortable about seeing this client, then you should offer telephone coaching only.

With experience, most coaches learn to observe the danger signals. Signing on for self-defence training might give you confidence, both in the consultation room and when walking home alone on a dark night It is also important to remember that you need to keep your self-defence skills training fresh in your mind by attending refresher courses, otherwise you may well have forgotten what to do when you need to use them.

If you genuinely find yourself worrying about your personal safety in an office on your own, then it will probably affect the quality of your work, and you may wish to think seriously about restricting your coaching work to telephone coaching only, or corporate work in a well-populated office environment.

Alternatives could be to find other coaches willing to share premises with you, or to respond to one of the various advertisements in professional journals with offers of room hire along similar lines. Even renting a room in a local accountant's or solicitor's office is a possibility to consider. More costly though this would be, it may resolve your concerns over personal safety and allow you to work free from this worry.

15

Time management

Most newly self-employed people in any profession vastly under-estimate the number of non-chargeable hours they must do to support their chargeable hours.

By "chargeable hours" we mean the number of actual fee-earning (bill-paying) up-front client hours that you do per day or per week. By "non-chargeable hours" we mean all the other efforts and paperwork that you need to make time for to ensure that you have clients, and that the practice runs professionally and smoothly.

Working with trainee coaches, we discovered that many envisage their practice time consisting of client sessions – either face-to-face or on the telephone – during the day, followed by a small amount of note-making, after which they close the office door and move on to their social and domestic life.

This is unlikely ever to be the case, even in the most successful practice, and it is where time management becomes important – finding a balance between bringing income into the business directly, and using the rest of your time as effectively as possible to ensure that the business not only stays afloat, but also expands and develops.

If you are marketing your services, you will need time to keep on top of it, in addition to work preparation, letter writing, telephoning, face-to-face meetings, invoicing, note-taking, record-keeping, stationery ordering, trying to fix a recalcitrant computer, research and CPD (continuous professional develop-ment) courses (and of course, the dreaded income tax return). Many freelance coaches (as well as freelancers in other areas) operate on the "wing and a prayer" principle that if they work hard and conscientiously, somehow it will all fit together.

Perhaps you will choose to limit your client workload to a set number of individual client sessions per week: the "keeping things simple" approach, which also keeps a neat structure that you can work within. However, if you wish to run a flourishing, full-time practice that includes lots of extra activities such as training, writing, corporate work etc., you will need to learn to manage your time very effectively to avoid work overload and burnout.

Kate Hinch, a time management trainer, advocates six principles of time good management (Hinch, 2002, email communication:

- Value your time. Don't fritter it away on pointless tasks – it is a precious commodity that needs to be well spent if you are to succeed.
- Analyse and prioritise tasks. Do not undertake tasks as they arrive on your desk, but think about their current importance in relation to other work you have to do.
- Know what to do – and what not to do. Have a task list that incorporates your prioritised workload. If other things creep in, be firm with yourself about leaving them alone.
- Say "no" when appropriate – and mean it. One of the hardest things to do, especially with a new business, is to turn work away. You may want to accept every piece of work that comes in to build the business up and to earn money. You may believe that turning work away means that it will be the last work you are ever offered, and that you will live to regret saying "no". You must learn to do so, or you may find yourself so swamped that you are not working effectively, or on the work areas you find most challenging and productive.
- Spend time to save time. In simple terms, doing things like spending a few minutes on note-taking immediately after the client has left is quicker than leaving it a day or so and then having to spend extra thinking time trying to recall exactly what the main points of the session were.
- Don't procrastinate – do it now. In other words, stop unbending those paperclips and gazing out of the window,

and start making those difficult telephone calls to clients whose session payments are outstanding.

If time management is proving to be a problem, or if you want to pre-empt problems before they arise, you need to look precisely at the amount of actual time you spend over, say, a week or a month on running your practice and the various tasks that involves. You need to discover the total number of hours these things take you. Depending on the result of this exercise, you may need to start prioritising your activities and get rid of or minimise the less productive activities.

We suggest that the easiest way of achieving this is to keep a diary record over, say, a two-week period. You need to keep a record of your income from your chargeable hours as well as the total number of hours you have spent on your business over the same period. When you have added all your activities together, divide your income by the hours concerned and this is your true hourly rate. You may get quite a shock when you do this, and want to reconsider your fee scales.

There is a wide variety of time management models, and perhaps one of the most widely known is Steven Covey's "time management matrix" (1992). Covey suggests dividing your "to do" list into four boxes:

1 Urgent and important
2 Important but not urgent
3 Urgent but not important
4 Neither important nor urgent.

You will not have too much difficulty differentiating between what goes into each category. For example in Box 1, "Urgent and important", go items such as the phone call you must make today to secure new business, the letter you need to write confirming a course attendance, the income tax return you need to have in the post by Friday and so on. These activities are very necessary and driven by a "here and now" urgency.

You may consider that this is the most important box to spend your time in, and may hang out there for most of your time. According to Covey, this is the wrong place to be.

He suggests that the most important box to spend time in is Box 2, "Important but not urgent", as this is where all your real development goals lie. In this box goes reading, research, learning new skills, marketing your practice, re-assessing your career goals and anything else that will develop both yourself and your business, but which doesn't need to be done today.

Box 3, "Urgent but not important", contains such things as paying a final demand for a newspaper bill or reaching the dry cleaner before it closes.

Box 4, "Neither important nor urgent", relates to things such as watching TV, unbending paperclips, social telephone calls, browsing round the shops etc.

Unless you spend as much time as you can working with items in Box 2, "Important but not urgent", it will be hard for your business to develop. While we tend to react to urgent matters, we take the initiative and are more pro-active with important matters.

Reflection issues

- How would you describe your time management skills?
- Which time management skills do you need to improve?
- If you procrastinate how could you choose to confront it?

Having read this section, what issues in it do you believe that you need to address?

How will you do this?

Issue	Action	By when?	Done?

By tackling these issues, what results have you achieved?

If you have been unable to tackle any of the issues you have listed, what has prevented you?

What do you need to do to rectify the situation?

16

What does it mean to be a professional coach?

Coaching as an emerging profession

In the past few years the coaching profession has moved forward from relative obscurity to a secure place in the field of personal development work. Many books are now published on the subject, and coaches are interviewed in magazines and national newspapers and asked to give professional views on any number of television series – especially the currently popular lifestyle make-over style of programme. From blue-chip companies to small businesses and individuals wanting to improve their lives, coaching is seen by many as the way forward.

In the 1980s, business consultants were regularly hired by companies to boost their flagging fortunes. The consultants created actions plans that the staff of the companies followed. One of the reasons that corporate coaching has gained in popularity is that it is the staff themselves who are encouraged to create their own actions plans – a much more powerful and enhancing strategy for developing a company's best resource.

As coaching has become more recognised and in demand, coaches themselves have learned to adopt more professional approaches to this exciting career. There are more training courses offering diverse coaching qualifications, professional bodies that coaches can become affiliated to, and a general raising of professional expectations from the purchasers of the service.

Why join a professional body?

The main advantages of becoming a member a professional association, especially for those in private practice, are as follows:

- It sets a standard of professionalism for your practice that will be welcomed by at least your more discerning clients.
- Through its journals, a professional body offers you the opportunity to keep in touch with the coaching world, the viewpoints of others, new information regarding practice ethics and essentials, books, courses and research findings.
- Each professional organisation has a code of ethics and practice that its members must abide by. This code of ethics actually offers the practitioner a series of guidelines for good practice while adding to your credibility with clients.
- Information lines at the organisation's headquarters will usually be able to help with the multitude of miscellaneous queries that crop up for coaches, from "Where can I find good insurance cover?" to "Can you let me know what other coaches there are in my geographical area?"
- For your clients, your membership offers the safety of a complaints procedure, should a client feel that the coaching has been unhelpful.
- Most professional bodies hold a public register of members, which enables potential clients to learn about your services.

There is presently no single professional body that is recognised as the gold standard for membership or accreditation but, nonetheless, there are one or two that offer you the opportunity, not only of membership, but also of accreditation, and this will give you more credibility and status with both clients and prospective clients. As the industry will almost certainly become more tightly regulated in the future, it could be well worth exploring these possibilities at this stage. Accreditation processes usually get harder, rather than easier, as a profession gains status.

As we write, there are a number of UK and international coaching organisations offering a variety of accreditations, or training with an accredited outcome. For example:

- Association for Coaching:
  http://www.associationforcoaching.com
- Association for Professional Executive Coaching and Supervision: http://www.apecs.uk.com
- The International Coach Federation:
  http://www.coachingfederation.org
- The International Association of Coaches:
  http://www.certifiedcoach.org

In our appendix we have provided additional details about these and other coaching bodies.

Professional expectations

At this point in time there is no legislation to prevent anyone setting up as a coach. However, in reality, if you do wish to develop a stable and reputable practice, clients will have a variety of professional expectations, and you need to be able to meet these expectations adequately as you build up your practice.

In early 2004, the University of Central England and Origin Consulting published *The Coaching Study 2004*, and within this they list an agreed set of criteria that the majority of organisations apply when selecting external coaches. It will be useful for you to consider these when marketing your own skills and experience. The criteria identified are:

- Coaching experience: length of time practised, environments, levels and situations.
- Track record: evidence of success and testimonials.
- Costs: fee levels and flexibility in payment terms.
- Having a structured approach: evidence of following a robust model, a tried-and-tested approach.
- Geographic coverage: mobility and flexibility to provide coaching wherever necessary.
- Line management experience: having worked in a variety of management roles.
- Knowledge of the organisation: understanding the unique requirements of the business/culture.

- Experience of the industry/sector: having worked in a similar organisation.
- Cultural fit: combines experience and personal style to fit the environment.
- Personal style: displays desired behaviours and congruent personal values.
- Adherence to professional standards: evidence of professionalism and awareness of ethical issues.
- Continuing professional development: evidence of on-going professional development activity.
- Supervision for the coach: access to regular supervision in support of their practice.
- Issue fit: has particular experience to support specific need.
- Scalability: adaptability to organisation's volume requirements.
- Quality of presentation/materials: displays a professional and impressive image.
- Coaching qualifications: relevant academic and/or professional accreditation.

Do not worry that all organisations will ask for all of these qualities. But knowing what they are, and matching them to your particular strengths (for example, you may be especially well qualified or experienced) will enable you to emphasise particular points during conversations and leave a positive impression of your skills and attributes. The bottom line is that there may well be some organisations for which your skills are not especially suited, and if you can acknowledge this and focus on those where you do have a "fit", you will generate far more work.

When you consider your goals for CPD, you would do well to regard this list as a blueprint, and plan over time to achieve at least the majority of the above professional expectations in order to enhance your business.

Contracting

You will enhance your professional standing by giving clients and potential clients as much written information about your services as you can. This information can also incorporate the essence of a contract between coach and client that you will both agree to, in order to make certain that quality of service is ensured for the client, and that the coach can maintain professional standards throughout his/her association with the client.

You may be so keen to develop a client base that the idea of a contract between yourself as the coach and the receiver of your services, the client, may be something you feel might frighten them away, by appearing too rigid, legally-driven and formal. However, it is in both of your interests to define the terms of your services at the start of your coaching relationship, to avoid possible nasty confrontations at a later date – or, at least, misunderstandings about the way in which your coaching service operates. A helpful way to go forward is not to use the word "contract" too freely, but rather to develop a client information sheet, and simply ask the client to sign it at the end to indicate that s/he agrees with, and will abide by, its contents.

It is important that you understand a little about the nature of a contract, as you may have to deal with many different types in your work, especially if you begin to develop corporate clients.

A contract between coach and client ensures that both parties are clear about the services offered and the individual responsibilities of each party. Keenan (1995) defines the first essential element of a contract as being the offer of something and its acceptance. Thus, the offer of coaching and its acceptance forms the basic coaching contract.

When a client gives you money for your services, this contract is legally binding. So what are the critical, "not to be missed" elements of a reasonable contract between client and coach? Is a verbal contract adequate? If written, how lengthy should it be before your client becomes too confused and anxious about it?

A verbal contract is just as legally binding as a written one – but much harder to remember and prove with regard to content, should it come to that. It is also asking a lot of clients at their first session to expect them to remember and absorb everything that they hear, even though it is familiar to you as you have gone through it so many times before. Therefore, a written contract makes much more sense for you both. The client has the opportunity to take it home and study it, and subsequently ask questions about areas they are not comfortable with. Where possible (i.e. time and the mail service allowing) we try to send this information out ahead of the first session, so that the client has advance knowledge of the practical elements of the service they are purchasing. This would be especially important if you are offering a telephone coaching service, as you may not have face-to-face contact with the client at any stage.

Take time to decide what you want to put in your contract, and review it regularly to ensure it represents your current practice. Circumstances are sure to arise which you had not expected and you will need to build these in as your experience increases. Share this information with your client and agree the elements of the contract, ensuring that the client understands those sections that are not open for negotiation.

As mentioned above, it is a good idea to produce a client information sheet which can also serve as your contract. This will give the client details of your specific coaching practice, and also give them a broader-based idea of what coaching is about, and hopefully encourage them to come to a positive decision to use your services. You will have similar information in your brochure, but in this instance the information is going to a client you have already made an initial appointment with. This information sheet can also contain all the information regarding the terms and conditions under which coaching is offered. It can be sent to the client together with a covering letter confirming the time of the appointment before they attend or telephone for the first session. By doing this you ensure that the client has the relevant information about what is expected of both parties. In addition, it shortens the contracting process when the client attends for his or her first session.

Some coaches, however, prefer to work through the contract together with the client, allowing the client to take a copy away following the first session in order to read it through again and ask any questions. Further, some coaches prefer to provide a contract which is "cast in concrete", simply asking the client to agree to the terms and conditions outlined.

It is actually extremely unlikely that you will ever need to test the legality of this contract. However, you may possibly have occasion to use the Small Claims Court, for example (discussed in more detail later in this book), and showing that you have listed all your terms and conditions, and that your client has agreed them, will be extremely helpful to your claim. It will also offer you protection should you be so unfortunate as to be sued by a client over an aspect of your service.

A sample client information sheet is shown in Form 16.1.

Some coaches may be concerned that an information sheet and subsequent contracting process is off-putting to the client. However, it is the view of the authors that the opportunity it offers to give the client a large amount of essential information at an early stage, as well as the sense of professionalism it projects, far outweighs these concerns.

It is important for the coach to refer to the contract and to go through its contents in a way that inspires a sense of working together, rather than simply reading out a list of rules. How you work through the contract with your client can also add to the coaching process.

While clients need to know about such issues as confidentiality, session times and fees by the start of the first session, everything else can wait until the first session ends, and you have decided to work together over a number of sessions.

If you are to work together you can then complete the contracting process by asking your client to complete a client details form (see Form 16.2 for an example). Once this has been completed, not only does it provide useful contact details, it also provides the evidence that your client has read, understood and agrees to the terms and conditions outlined.

As with all paperwork, if you are coaching by telephone you can send these forms through the post to your client ahead of time.

Whether you ask the client to sign the contract or you both sign it is a personal decision.

There are certain things that your clients themselves need to consider, and it will actually add to your professional status if you are the one to point these out to them. Palmer and Szymanska (1994) suggest certain checks that a (would-be) client should consider and pertinent examples of these are listed below. You might like to consider how you could respond to them, and whether there are any gaps in your expertise relating to your clients' expectations. There may also be other items you would want to add to this list.

Form 16.1   **Sample client information sheet**

Axis Coaching Associates
11 Anywhere Street, Anywhere, London SE9 TNR
Tel: 020 8841 4712, Fax: 020 8841 2009
Email: axis@anywhere.com

Client information sheet

Training and experience
I hold a BA (Hons) in Business Management, a Diploma in
Coaching and a Certificate in Business Development Coaching. I
also engage in a minimum of 30 hours Continued Professional
Development annually. I set up Axis Coaching Associates in
1997. Prior to this I worked as a change management trainer for
a major pharmaceutical company, which involved me in
motivating staff and helping them set and develop targets and
goals that would enhance their personal and career
development. I currently work with a wide variety of clients,
both in corporate settings and individually, both face-to-face
and via telephone coaching.

How coaching can help you
Coaching can help you to experience life as you ideally wish to.
For some people, it can literally change their lives. With a
supportive coach, you will be able to make improved judgements
of situations, make better choices, set challenging but
achievable goals and become a more effective decision-maker.
    Coaching will teach you to work on your self-development
in a way that is personally beneficial to you. You may wish to
improve a specific situation in your life and to achieve specific
goals. You may wish to learn new ways of thinking about and
approaching situations, so that you achieve more positive
results. Coaching will offer a combination of questioning,
listening, feedback and goal-setting. Your coach will offer a
unique kind of support – focussing totally on your own position,
and giving you a genuine commitment to your well-being.
    Coaching adopts the principle that we are all responsible
for our own well-being, which is a positive concept in that it

means, by default, that we have the power and influence to change our situations if we can work out how to do so. Your coach will help you to clarify and understand your present situation, encourage you to develop new ways of dealing with this, and help you to work on a positive action plan to achieve the result you want. The results for you should include:

- increased motivation and resourcefulness
- a better sense of personal direction and what is really important in your life
- improvement in your interpersonal relationships and ability to influence people positively
- improved personal awareness and effectiveness.

Confidentiality

The relationship between client and coach is crucial to the success of the coaching process. Because the relationship is based on trust and openness, all information disclosed will be confidential and no client details will be given to any third party without your permission (although such confidentiality can only be offered within accepted legal boundaries). I will keep brief notes on our work together and you are entitled to see these at any time if you so wish.

The coaching process

I normally offer all prospective clients an assessment interview, which gives both of us the opportunity to consider whether we wish to work together. It is important that you feel comfortable with your coach and that your coach feels able to work with you. If we decide to work together we will arrange to meet, or speak on the telephone, for an agreed number of sessions, usually arranged over monthly periods.

There is no obligation to take up all the sessions arranged and you are free to terminate your coaching at any time. A review session will take place at the end of the agreed number of sessions, where we will jointly assess your progress and what further action, if any, may be needed.

Coaching sessions, both face-to-face and by telephone, are time limited, and if you are late arriving or calling we will still terminate at the usual time so as not to delay the next client. Where we are working by telephone, I will be ready for your call at the agreed time, and you will initiate the call.

Availability

My working hours are 8.30am to 6.30pm Monday to Friday. I can offer evening sessions on Tuesdays and Thursdays between 6.30pm and 9.30pm. I do not normally work at weekends.

Contact

There may be times when you wish to contact me between sessions when I may be unavailable for various reasons. If so, you are most welcome to leave a message on my confidential voice mail service, and I will get back to you as soon as it is possible for me to do so. If I need to contact you I will simply leave my name and telephone number should you be unavailable.

Fees

Individual coaching session (60 minutes)	£–
Four one-hour sessions per month: monthly price	£– (this can be discounted against a single session price)
Three one-hour sessions per month: monthly price	£–

Corporate packages are available on request – please ask for our brochure on this service.

Payment for an individual session is made at the time of the session. Where a number of sessions are booked, payment should be made at the time of, or prior to, the first session. Organisations are invoiced on a monthly basis or at the end of a given contract period. Fees are subject to annual review.

A minimum of 24 hours notice is required for cancelled appointments otherwise the full fee is payable. Non-payment of fees may result in legal action being taken.

Travel instructions
National Rail: Anywhere Station
Buses: 54, 89, 75, 108
Parking: Parking spaces usually available outside the premises

In the experience of the authors, giving a client a copy of such information (possibly together with the client information sheet, discussed previously) promotes a sense of the coach's professionalism. Being encouraged to be aware – ahead of their first conversation with the coach – of professional issues they should consider, helps clients understand the basics of the coaching relationship before they begin coaching sessions.

An information sheet such as the one illustrated in Form 16.3 may be helpful.

Continuous professional development

Continuous professional development (CPD) will be a part of any good coach's planning, and expanding your skills should include continually building upon general basic expectations for professional coaching. At present, CPD is regarded as your own responsibility, rather than a legal requirement, but think in terms of 30 hours, plus or minus, per annum, and keep written records of your development. Attending seminars, courses and reading appropriate books, articles and journals can all count towards CPD. In addition some organisations offer a range of online coaching discussions or telephone conferences with coaching experts. We've enjoyed and benefited from using all of these methods of CPD.

Form 16.2 **Sample client details form**

Axis Coaching Associates
11 Anywhere Street, Anywhere, London SE9 TNR
Tel: 020 8841 4712, Fax: 020 8841 2009
Email: axis@anywhere.com

Client details form

Personal details

Surname: _____

Given names: _____

Address: _____

_____

_____

Postcode: _____

Tel. no(s):   (Home): _____ (Work): _____

Mobile: _____ Pager: _____

Email: _____

Date of birth: _____

How did you hear of this service? _____

Type of coaching preferred
(face-to-face, by telephone): _____

Preferred times for sessions
(am, pm, evenings, particular days): _____

Anticipated start date for coaching: _____

My signature below confirms that I have read and understood
all the information detailed in the Client Information Sheet
supplied to me and that I agree to abide by the terms and
conditions outlined therein.

Signed: _____

Date: _____

Form 16.3   **Sample information sheet**

Axis Coaching Associates
11 Anywhere Street, Anywhere, London SE9 TNR
Tel: 020 8841 4712, Fax: 020 8841 2009
Email: axis@anywhere.com

Issues for the client to consider

Given below are some suggestions for points you may wish to consider or raise at, or prior to, your initial interview. You may wish to add more to your list:

- To discuss your expectations of coaching and the goals you want to achieve.
- To ask about fees and discuss the frequency and estimated duration of coaching.
- To arrange regular review sessions with your coach to evaluate your progress.
- To be cautious about entering into a long-term coaching contract unless you are satisfied that it will be beneficial to you.
- Other points/questions that you may wish to consider or discuss.

_____

_____

_____

If you do not have a chance to discuss the above points during your first session, discuss them at the next possible opportunity.

General issues
Coaching is based on a close personal relationship between client and coach, but there are, nonetheless, boundaries (some obvious, others less so) that you should be aware of, and you should understand where these boundaries begin and end in a fully professional relationship. Please be aware of the points raised below:

- Avoid being coached by somebody you personally know as the process of coaching could later impact upon your relationship.
- If your coach wishes to socialise with you or become more intimate, carefully consider the possible consequences to you personally. This behaviour would normally be considered as unprofessional on the part of the coach.
- Coach self-disclosure can be useful and pertinent. However, if the coach discussing his/her own situation dominates sessions, this will not be helpful to you, and you should raise this with the coach.
- If you feel uncomfortable at any time within the session, discuss this with the coach. It is easier to resolve issues as and when they arise.
- If you feel that the coach is controlling or dominating the conversation, tell the coach this.
- Do not accept gifts from your coach. (This does not, of course, apply to relevant coaching material.)
- If your coach proposes a change in venue without good reason (e.g. from his or her office to their home) do not agree.
- You have the right to terminate your coaching sessions at any time you wish.

(Adapted with permission from Palmer & Szymanska, 1994)

Reflection issues

- What type of contracting process do you want to put in place and what paperwork do you require?
- What are your views about dual relationships with clients? If you are a life coach in private practice is there any justification in coaching people you know?
- Do you think that CPD is relevant for you?

Having read this section, what issues in it do you believe that you need to address?

How will you do this?

Issue	Action	By when?	Done?

By tackling these issues, what results have you achieved?

If you have been unable to tackle any of the issues you have listed, what has prevented you?

What do you need to do to rectify the situation?

17

Coaching and the law

Legal requirements

We are fortunate in the UK that we do not yet have quite such a culture of litigation, enthusiastically aided and abetted by lawyers, that pervades the United States. However, the situation is changing and we are fast catching up – as can be seen from TV advertisements for "No win, no fee" claims and, "Where there's blame, there may be a claim" etc. (what these advertisements do not say is what proportion of any payout is taken by the lawyers and others!).

In addition, when you accept money to undertake a task such as coaching in your own practice, the various laws protecting the consumer come into play. When you were in employment, your employer ensured considerable protection for you against any claims brought. When you are a private practitioner, that protection goes completely out of the window. If you take money for your services the law will presume that you are working in a professional capacity and have the skills required to do so. If a claim is made it will be made against the individual practitioner, which means you. We have spoken already about the importance of personal liability insurance. Do take this seriously and ensure that you are fully covered, or you may lose not only your business but your home as well – the proverbial "shirt off your back".

We will start by looking at some of the legal requirements for self-employed coaches and some of the equally "grey" areas that fall under this heading.

Who can coach legally in the UK?

Currently there is no legislation to prevent anybody from putting up a name plaque on their door and practising as a coach in the UK. However, this does not make it right! We recommend at least attending a basic six-day training programme and on-going supervision before you practise as a coach. Of course, some readers in their previous jobs as managers may have been a coach or mentor to staff. They may need less training. You will need to assess this yourself, perhaps with help from a more experienced coach or supervisor.

Confidentiality and the law

Coaches normally go out of their way to stress the confidential nature of their services to clients. However, in reality, no-one bar a solicitor or barrister has the right to total confidentiality – not even doctors. The law can demand far more from practitioners: you can be subpoenaed for reasons including court action, potentially dangerous clients and professional impropriety. It is therefore important to be aware of what information you may be required to share, and in what circumstances, so that you can prepare your administration and note-taking with this in mind.

Courts of law may need to see a coach's notes and/or any material that is related to the client, for example tapes, questionnaires, letters etc. (Scroggins et al., 1997; Palmer, 2002). While it is extremely unlikely that you would find yourself in this position, you will need to bear this possibility in mind, as it is likely to affect such matters as the content of your note-taking (see the section on note-taking).

Were you ever to find yourself in the unfortunate situation where a client you have been working with faces prosecution of any sort, your case notes may be required to substantiate the facts of a situation. As a self-employed coach, you are not obliged by law to reveal such evidence, unless a court order is taken out requiring you to submit it. It would be helpful for you to think about your policy regarding confidentiality in advance of any such difficulties arising. You may perhaps wish to put some wording in your client information sheet that clarifies at what point in the legal process your confidentiality agreement with the client takes second place to due process of the law.

We can only cover a limited number of your possible legal obligations due to your position as a coach in this book, and we strongly recommend that you research the subject further so that you are confident that you are not in breach of the law when an unexpected situation arises.

Taping sessions

As well as taking notes, you may either occasionally or regularly tape your coaching sessions, either so that you can review the session yourself at a later time, or to give a copy to your client that they may listen to again, perhaps in the car or at home, to remind themselves of the most important points discussed.

While this is an excellent idea where both the coach and client agree, from a legal point of view there are considerations.

In circumstances that would be both unfortunate and unlikely (but nonetheless possible) these tapes could be requested in a court of law, and precedent means that you would have to submit them if asked to do so (Scroggins et al., 1997; Palmer, 2002). Beyond this, you need to consider where you could keep such tapes safely and how long you would keep them for, and possibly inform the client of these decisions. Do remember that it is your responsibility to be aware of any changes the government might make to the laws of confidentiality and access. Relevant professional journals will usually provide you with such information or at least alert you to such changes, and this is where belonging to a professional body becomes helpful.

Using the Small Claims Court

While hopefully you will not incur bad debts – or at least, not too many of them – you will need to decide how far you wish to pursue these, if and when they arise. One way of doing so, as mentioned earlier, is through the Small Claims Court. The first advantage of taking this route is that, quite probably, once your client has been informed that you are proceeding in this way, he/she will settle the bill and save a lot of further aggravation. The second is that it is fairly cost-free, because solicitors will not be involved.

The small claims track is designed to provide a procedure whereby claims of not more than £5,000 in value can be dealt with quickly and at minimal cost to the parties. The intention is to make the procedure as simple as possible, without calling on solicitors. The reason for this is that the costs that can be recovered by a successful party are extremely limited, and it is therefore considered uneconomic for solicitors to represent the parties in a small claim. You will be given clear directions as to what paperwork you need to supply, the hearing itself will be very informal and, if all parties agree, the court can deal with the claim without a hearing at all. In other words, a court could make a decision based on the statements of case and documents submitted, rather than by your having to turn up to give oral evidence.

As mentioned above, the costs which can be recovered in a small claims case are limited, and include only fixed costs attributable to issuing the claim, any court fees paid and sums to represent travelling expenses and – importantly for you – loss of earnings.

Some coaches are concerned that taking a client to a Small Claims Court would be a break in confidentiality. However, this is where the client information sheet comes into its own, as it states that "non-payment of fees may result in legal action being taken".

18

How competent are you?

Minimum training requirements

As we write this book (2004), there are no minimum training requirements for coaches. There is even an argument that becoming a good coach is a skill that develops over time through experience, and that the possession of particular personal strengths will mean that you have a gift for developing and helping others to achieve their goals.

This may be true, and there is no doubt that coaching as a career is best suited to certain types of people. However, this is a young industry and, as it grows, professional coaching organisations will continue to develop standards that will serve as a yardstick for the public – your clients – and enable them to become selective in their choice of professional.

We assume that many of you reading this book are already experienced coaches. However, there will be some readers for whom this is just a possible career option at present, and the issue of qualifications will no doubt influence any decisions that you make about it.

The authors thoroughly recommend that you obtain – if you do not already have – some form of coaching qualification, and make gaining further qualifications part of your CPD. If you have already had a variety of senior management roles that have involved "bringing on" other staff, then this experience may well stand you in good enough stead, initially at least. If this is not the case, we recommend that you starting working towards qualifications before you start your practice.

It is hard for us to recommend specific organisations offering courses, as there is a proliferation of them all over the country.

They range from short courses, distance learning, internet options etc. to year-long attendance at college leading to a diploma qualification.

Here are a few suggestions (of many) if you already hold a first degree:

- Wolverhampton University, MA in Coaching and Mentoring: http://www.wlv.ac.uk
- Portsmouth University, MA in Coaching: http://www.port.ac.uk
- Sheffield Hallam University, MSc in Mentoring and Coaching: http://www.shu.ac.uk/schools/sbf/coursepg.html
- Oxford Brookes University, MA in Coaching and Mentoring Practice: http://www.brookes.ac.uk/education/macoachment.html
- The Centre for Coaching offers a range of certificate and diploma programmes in coaching, psychological coaching, coaching psychology and speciality coaching accredited by Middlesex University at graduate and postgraduate levels: http://www.centreforcoaching.com

If you would like to compare courses at a variety of different levels, an excellent website listing these is the Coaching and Mentoring Network: http://www.coachingnetwork.org.uk

As with all young professions, the professional bodies will tighten up and make the process of accreditation more rigorous as the years go by. Our advice would be to become professionally established as soon as possible from the point of view of qualifications and accreditations, as the task will become more difficult over time – and you may even find that you cannot practise at all without these things.

At present, different colleges and organisations offer their own qualifications in coaching. You will need to consider how you wish to undertake your training, and what is most important to you. As well as our suggestions above, your simplest way of finding out what courses are on offer is to use the internet (http://www.google.co.uk/life coaching, for example, will yield pages of suitable sites). Here are some questions you might consider when evaluating the different options:

- What is the reputation of the college? How long has it been in existence, and for how long has it run coaching courses?
- How will you be studying: regular attendance, distance learning or computer conferencing? What is your preference?
- How comprehensive is the course and how long a period of time does it run for? You may prefer to devote a great deal of time in a short period to study, or you may prefer the "little and often" approach over a longer period.
- Does it primarily focus on an academic approach, or a practical one?
- Will you be learning solely the skills of coaching, or will you also be offered advice on actually setting up a coaching business?
- How much time can you give to further study when you are in a work situation and possibly trying to develop a new business?

Your choice of course will also depend on the type of work you expect to be involved in – do you plan to work mainly with individual clients or, perhaps, to develop business performance coaching? Following a basic certification, you can pick up these specialities.

Continuous professional development

While not yet mandatory in the field of coaching, it is an excellent idea to get into the habit of developing your skills and knowledge on a regular basis. Decide on a certain number of hours annually – say 30, which is often the amount recommended by professional bodies – and commit to whatever form of training you feel is beneficial to you (even book reading counts!) to ensure that you keep your skills up-to-date.

One of the authors has made it a policy to undertake one certificated training in coaching or a related area annually. This has not only helped with increasing the coach's knowledge and ability to help clients but it has also added to the credibility of the coach in terms of perceived capability by clients and others.

Another form of professional development is to undertake professional coaching yourself, where you are the client. On courses you take this may certainly be a requirement – especially those at a more advanced level – and you will learn a great deal from being on the other side of the fence from time to time. This requirement does make sense, if for no other reason than that it is important to see and learn from coaching in action, and understand what being a client feels like.

This is a personal decision, and not in any way mandatory (except, as we have mentioned, on certain training courses) but is certainly worth considering.

Supervision

Supervision is a formal process in which the coach meets with a more experienced colleague in order to receive support and evaluation of the quality of the coaching work undertaken. It may reflect on particular client issues or the more general elements of best practice in coaching, so that the process is one of both evaluation and learning.

As yet, there are no specific guidelines for the frequency of supervision, but we suggest an average of one session per month, lasting between 60 and 90 minutes, with an option to increase this where it might be necessary.

Supervision is not presently mandatory with all professional bodies, although coaching supervision should be a "given" in your coaching development and an investment in the well-being of your clients. In particular, the British Psychological Society Special Group in Coaching Psychology recommends that its members in training may benefit from supervision. And even as experienced coaches we have still found supervision beneficial for ourselves.

You can attend a one-day coaching supervision course at Oxford Brookes University: email wiecmp@brookes.ac.uk for details. The Centre for Coaching runs a short course too: http://www.centreforcoaching.com

Evaluation of your service

In simple terms, evaluation and auditing means accounting for what you do and why you do it. If you have previously been employed in a public company, you may be familiar with the term "audit". We are not talking here about purely financial outcomes. Rather, we are also referring to an evaluation of your service which will (hopefully) indicate positive client outcomes. The term now commonly used in these instances is "evidence-based practice".

Of course, when you work for yourself you do not need to measure and evaluate positive client outcomes except on your own behalf. However, it is important if you want to ensure that your practice is successful and that you are developing it along the right lines.

In private practice, accounting can take many forms:

- Reviewing your own on-going development as a coach.
- Ensuring that your qualifications are up-to-date and sufficient for the work that you undertake.
- Continually ensuring that your practice is run in a professional and cost-efficient manner.
- Inviting client feedback either formally or informally as a measure of the success of your coaching.
- Monitoring the number of sessions needed per client to achieve the results they want.
- Finally, of course, reviewing your net income and hopefully seeing this increasing over time for positive reasons.

Auditing your practice can either be an on-going task, or based on an annual "competence audit" where you review your procedures for running your practice generally. Such an audit could cover record-keeping systems, IT use, marketing, finances, evaluation of skills etc.

To complete these evaluation processes it will be important to set yourself goals, so that you know at the start of the year what you hope to achieve by the end of it. You may then find it helpful to break these targets down into smaller goals, to be reached within shorter time periods – say, six months, a month, or even a week.

Thus you have the opportunity to review whether you are on track, or need to re-evaluate and re-set your goals. Make sure that your goals are written down, clearly, on the left side of a sheet of paper, or in a notebook. On the right hand side of the paper, write down the action that you are committed to take in order to achieve that goal. For example, if you write down,

"Increase number of clients", "Work shorter hours" and "Improve record-keeping", alongside each you must write down exactly what you need to do and how you plan to achieve this and by when.

Client feedback

It obviously makes sense, if you wish to develop your practice, to find out from clients what skills they have found most helpful in achieving their own goals. This will help you to develop best practice. You can do this by using a simple client evaluation sheet, and we give an example of what this might look like in Form 18.1.

It is not particularly valid for you, as the coach, to make a judgement on the success or failure of your coaching with a client. The important marker is how the *client* sees it. This will really tell you what you have achieved. In simplistic terms, it is about the clients feeling that they have achieved the results that they wanted, and therefore leave you with their goals realised.

Form 18.1   **Sample client evaluation sheet**

Axis Coaching Associates
11 Anywhere Street, Anywhere, London SE9 TNR
Tel: 020 8841 4712, Fax: 020 8841 2009
Email: axis@anywhere.com

Client satisfaction questionnaire

Your views are very important in helping us monitor the quality of the coaching work we undertake. Any information you provide will be treated as confidential.

Using a scale of 0–8 (0 = very poor and 8 = excellent) please rate the following:

Initial contact
1) How well was your initial enquiry dealt with?
   (e.g. efficiency, helpfulness etc.)

   0 1 2 3 4 5 6 7 8

2) How useful did you find the client information sent to you?

   0 1 2 3 4 5 6 7 8

The coaching environment
3) Where we have worked on a face-to-face basis, how would you rate the coaching environment?
   (e.g. accessibility, room standard, parking facilities etc.)

   0 1 2 3 4 5 6 7 8

The coach
4) How competent did you consider your coach to be?
   (e.g. a good understanding of the issues, easy to talk to, skilled etc.)

   0 1 2 3 4 5 6 7 8

5) What coaching skills did you find most helpful in achieving your goals?

   _____

_____

_____

_____

6) Was there any area of the service that you felt was not as helpful to you as you would have wished?

_____

_____

_____

_____

Your progress
Using the rating scale 0–8 (0 = "failing to achieve my goals" and 8 = "successful in achieving my goals") please rate the following:

7) Before you started coaching how would you have rated yourself?
   (e.g. uncertain of what you wanted from life and how to get it)

   0 1 2 3 4 5 6 7 8

8) After the coaching, how would you rate yourself?
   (e.g. able to define goals and achieve the results you want)

   0 1 2 3 4 5 6 7 8

Any other comments

_____

_____

_____

_____

Thank you for taking the time to complete this questionnaire.
Please return in the s.a.e. provided to the address above.

19

Keeping records

Note-taking

Note-taking – keeping a written record of your coaching sessions with clients – is vital to the professionalism of your service.

Your client needs to feel confident that you are making notes that you will be re-reading before the start of each session. You will be showing the client your commitment to him/her and also your professionalism, by providing continuity between sessions and being ready to move forward with the client towards his/her goals. It may be that some clients will only speak with you once a month, and it will be impossible for you to remember the contents of the previous session without reviewing what you worked on together.

We would temper our recommendation to take notes with a proviso – don't take too many! First, this can be an onerous task. Second, if you choose to take notes during the coaching session, rather than at the end of it, you may miss something important that your client is telling you while you are busy scribing. And third, when you get the file out prior to your next session with the same client, you have too much to try to read and absorb before speaking with him/her.

So what is the best format for note-taking? This will be decided by asking: What is the purpose (or purposes) of keeping client records?

The most basic details – name, address and telephone number – are vital in case you need to change your meeting time at short notice (this information may already be available on the client details form). In addition to this you might also want to keep your clients' telephone numbers with you, perhaps by using a code in your diary or personal organiser. After all, you could find yourself on a station platform following an unexpected series of train cancellations with a client due to attend or telephone.

Apart from acting as an *aide memoir*, note-taking allows the coach to record considered views about what has happened in the session. As your caseload builds, you will find it more difficult to recall individual discussions with each client, and the stage in the coaching process that you have reached with them. Meanwhile, each client will be extremely mindful of exactly where they are at, and will not appreciate your not being at exactly that point with them. If you have appropriate notes, you can verify what a client has told you – sometimes a client will be certain that they have already mentioned something, and feel disappointed that you seem to have forgotten this fact. Being able to refer to your notes, you will be able to clarify that this is not in fact the case.

Also, some clients may return to you at a later stage, either with further situations they need to work on or perhaps for a "booster" session. It is obviously helpful if you can easily remind yourself of previous work you did with these clients.

As has already been mentioned in an earlier section, there is a faint possibility that you may at some point be legally required to submit either your notes, or a report on your notes, to a court of law.

We suggest that whatever style of note-keeping you choose to follow, you ensure it is consistent. Your notes will, ideally, record all the practical information on the client that you need.

We have already mentioned the possibility of taping the session, and this can often be an excellent idea. However, we suggest that the taping be additional to note-taking and not an alternative. We, ourselves, have occasionally found that, for some reason, the recording has either not come out well or not come out at all! So relying on electronics alone may not be a good idea.

A practical point: do ensure that you are well prepared for note-taking before the start of your session. Ensure that you have the client's file out, that you have reviewed where you are at this time, and that you have a pen or pencil to hand as well as a notepad or any specific client forms that you work with. Place these by the telephone if the client is ringing you, or on your desk if you are working face-to-face. It appears extremely unprofessional to have to hold up the session while you search around for these things with the client either with you, or hanging on to the telephone waiting for you to return.

Supporting documentation

In addition to your note-taking, you will very often build up a file of miscellaneous documents for each client, which you will need to keep carefully, safely and confidentially. You may, for example, wish to keep a separate client sheet recording such things as the person's basic details, start date, session times and session payments – how they paid, whether there are any fees outstanding, whether they have been invoiced and whether you have given them a receipt.

You may receive letters from your client or write letters to him/her. You may give them résumés of their goals and achievements. You may ask your clients to fill in assessment questionnaires. They may give you copies of work they have done outside the session, or other documentation that they would like you to see. In this regard, we recommend the early purchase of a small desktop photocopier, as soon as your practice can afford it.

The Data Protection Act

It is important that you make yourself familiar with the stipulations of the Data Protection Act. This was most recently updated in 1998; you can check the present regulations, and keep abreast of any further changes, at http://www.dataprotection. gov.uk. The Data Protection Registrar is usually very helpful, and in an attempt to make the process as simple as possible will complete your form for you so that all you have to do is check it and pay the annual registration fee.

In legal terms, professional codes of practice are not necessarily recognised in a court of law. While they do carry some weight in some courts, it is important to ensure that you primarily adhere to the Data Protection Act. However, from an ethical point of view, where you agree to work within the code of ethics and practice of a professional body, you will need to adhere to the guidelines laid out by them in addition to, and where they are not in conflict with, the Data Protection Act.

The important point to keep in mind, therefore, is that these ethical requirements do not necessarily fully cover your legal requirements. You are under further obligation to ensure that you fulfil these as well, in case of investigation.

Safe-keeping of records

So what constitutes safe-keeping in relation to written notes and other documentation?

There are two main considerations:

- Physical safe-keeping of records – against fire or theft, for example.
- Confidential safe-keeping of records – against their being read, or otherwise used, by third parties.

Physical safe-keeping is likely to take the form of a locked cabinet, and you need to think about where to keep the keys and the need for a second set just in case the first set is lost. These must also be kept confidentially, somewhere known only to you (and hidden well enough not to be stumbled across by anyone else) and one other named person. It is quite common, if your private practice is run from your home, to consider the garage as useful storage space – which indeed it is. However, you will need to think about the security aspect of this. Many of us store quite valuable items in our garages, and yet it can be one of the easiest parts of our homes for a thief to break into. While it is unlikely that coaching files would be of interest, it is still ethically important for you to ensure that they are, again, locked away here, with key(s) in a safe, confidential place. You could use a small portable lockable system in the office for current client notes and a standard lockable four-drawer filing cabinet in the garage for notes about clients you are no longer coaching.

What would happen to your files if you were not there? Who else knows where you keep your files? While on the one hand you are encouraged to be as discreet as possible with regard to their physical whereabouts, on the other hand, should anything happen to you, someone else must be able to "rescue" these files and ensure their destruction or safe-keeping. Whoever you give this information to, ensure that they have a set of written instructions as to where your files are kept, where the keys are kept and to whom he or she may reveal this information in order to ensure their care. This same person may also be willing confidentially to keep a regularly up-dated list of the telephone numbers of your current clients. Again, should you be involved in, for example, an accident, you may need someone you can trust to make urgent contact with clients in order to inform them of this.

The possibility of human error such as failing to lock the cabinet, or leaving a file on view, means it is important to ensure that you do not leave clients' personal details – name, contact address, telephone number etc. – in the same place as your case notes. While many of your clients will not feel a particular need for secrecy about their coaching sessions, some may, for a variety of different reasons, so it is simpler to assume that all clients want complete confidentiality, rather than make subjective judgements about this which can lead you into unprofessional casualness about file storage.

Use a code for each client on the case notes file, and keep a separate folder (or card index file) that lists his or her personal details and links him or her to the right case notes. It is a similar principle to keeping your bank card pin number in a different place to the card itself, and it goes without saying that this list must also be kept under lock and key, or otherwise securely stored.

How long should you retain client files? In fact, there is no particular law or legal requirement that specifies the exact period for keeping these files. However, the Law Society recommends that a period of six years plus one year (for safety) after the last contact with the client is a good standard benchmark.

After this period, you may get rid of the files. We suggest the following:

• Consider keeping your client's initial assessment sheet just in case you wish to refer to it for any reason.

- If you have access to a shredder, shred everything else to ensure efficient and complete disposal. If not then you could burn the notes to ensure they cannot be accidentally read by anyone else.

As you progress, you will devise your own best practice for storage of papers and your ethical and legal responsibility towards this, which will be dependent on your working environment and the system you personally find the most efficient and valuable.

Reflection issues

- Do you think it is unprofessional not to maintain records or notes of your coaching sessions?
- What note-keeping structure do you currently use and does it need amending in any way?
- Do you have a system for dealing with issues such as client documentation etc?

Having read this section, what issues in it do you believe that you need to address?

How will you do this?

Issue	Action	By when?	Done?

By tackling these issues, what results have you achieved?

If you have been unable to tackle any of the issues you have listed, what has prevented you?

What do you need to do to rectify the situation?

20

Referral issues for coaches

At some point in your career, it is likely that you will come across a client or clients with whom, for a variety of reasons, you cannot work. In such cases, the option of onward referral can provide a solution, both for you and for the client needing help.

The most likely reason for onward referral is that the client is looking for a specialist in a particular area that is not your forte. There are several different specialisations, the most common being relationships, wealth, health, spiritual and career issues. If you work as a general coach, and are not yet especially experienced in the particular area that the client is asking for, s/he will regard you as both courteous and professional if you are able to refer her/him on to someone who specifically works in this area.

It is, therefore, a good idea to build a referral list of specialist coaches who are, ideally, known to you, and whom you can recommend.

If clients are very distressed over an issue in their life or are suffering from clinical depression or anxiety, they are more likely to benefit from counselling, psychotherapy or, in some cases, medication. This may become apparent when first speaking to them, during your first coaching session or perhaps later. It is important to let them know that you are not rejecting them but different skills may be required to help them in this instance. The appendix includes contact details for the main counselling and psychotherapy bodies with registers of members.

You may also wish to refer clients on for the positive reason that you already have a full case-load. In this instance, you should have a list of general coaches to whom you can pass the client on. Again, ideally, they should be coaches known to you and whom you would recommend.

Finally, you may occasionally get enquiries from potential clients who fail to understand the nature of coaching and what it actually offers. They perhaps need a different sort of help and, again, it is professional and courteous to be able to point them in the direction of an individual or organisation which would be appropriate for them.

You never know when there may be benefits to you from this type of approach. Apart from offering alternative assistance to potential clients, their impression of you will be a good one, and they may eventually recommend their friends to you, who will turn out to be ideal clients for your business.

Postscript

You may now have finished reading this book. Some of you may believe that you are now well prepared to start the exciting and challenging journey of private practice. However, some of you may still feel concerned that it could be too much of a challenge. This is understandable. You may wish to spend more time in the planning phase and receive some professional guidance too.

We have attempted to cover the main areas involved in a coaching practice, including the personal issues that can create additional stress for us if we are not prepared to meet the internal and external challenges. This book has applied the self-coaching model whereby we encourage you, the reader, to plan, prepare and then act. The action can be taken alone or with the support of colleagues, professionals, family and friends. By breaking down the tasks involved in setting up in private practice into small manageable steps, the overall goals become easier.

We do not believe that we need to wish you good luck on your journey as we have found that hard work and practice seems to bring its own good luck. Do let us know how you progress in setting up and running your private practice.

Having read this book, what issues in it do you believe that you need to address?

How will you do this?

Issue	Action	By when?	Done?

By tackling these issues, what results have you achieved?

If you have been unable to tackle any of the issues you have listed, what has prevented you?

What do you need to do to rectify the situation?

References

Barrow, P. (2001) *The Best-Laid Business Plans: How to Write Them, How to Pitch Them*. London, Virgin Business Guides.

Caird, S. (1993) What do Psychological Tests Suggest About Entrepreneurs? *Journal of Managerial Psychology*, Vol. 8, No. 6, 11–20.

Cooper, C. L. & Palmer, S. (2000) *Conquer Your Stress*. London, Chartered Institute of Personnel and Development.

Covey, S. (1992) *The Seven Habits of Highly Effective People*. London, Simon and Schuster.

Drake, S. (2001) *Freelancing for Dummies*. New York, Hungry Minds Inc.

Fairley, G. & Stout, C. (2004) *Getting Started in Personal and Executive Coaching*. New Jersey, Wiley.

Gordon, L. (1984) *Survey of Personal Values (Examiner's Manual)*. Iowa, Science Research Asociates.

Howard, S. (1999) *Creating a Successful CV*. London, Dorling Kindersley.

Keenan, D. (1995) *English Law*. London, Pitman.

Martin, C. (2001) *The Coaching Handbook*. Carmarthen, Crown House.

McMahon, G. (1994) *Setting Up Your Own Private Practice in Counselling and Psychotherapy*. Cambridge, National Extension College.

McMullin, R. E. (1986) *Handbook of Cognitive Techniques*. New York, Norton.

Palmer, S. (2002) Confidentiality: A Case Study. In P. Jenkins (ed.), *Legal Issues in Counselling and Psychotherapy*, pp. 15–20. London, Sage.

Palmer, S., Cooper, C. & Thomas, K. (2003) *Creating a Balance: Managing Stress*. London, British Library.

Palmer, S. & Dryden, W. (1995) *Counselling for Stress Problems*. London, Sage.

Palmer, S. & Neenan, M. (1998) Double Imagery Procedure. *The Rational Emotive Behaviour Therapist*, Vol. 6, No. 2, 89–92.

Palmer, S. & Strickland, L. (1996) *Stress Management: A Quick Guide*. Dunstable, Folens.

Palmer, S. & Szymanska, K. (1994) How to Avoid Being Exploited in Counselling and Psychotherapy. *Counselling*, Vol. 5, No. 1, 24.

Palmer, S. & Whybrow, A. (2004) *Coaching Training Manual*. London, Centre for Coaching.

Scoggins, M., Litton, R. & Palmer, S. (1997) Confidentiality and the Law. *Counselling, Journal of the British Association for Counselling*, Vol. 8, No. 4, 258–262.

Truman, M. (1997) *Teach Yourself Book-Keeping and Accounting for your Small Business* (Teach Yourself Series). London, British Institute of Management.

Whiteley, J. (2002) *Small Business Tax Guide*. London, How To Reference.

Recommended reading

Legal and ethical issues

Clayton, P. (2001) *Law for the Small Business* (Business Enterprise Guides). London, Kogan Page.

Professional issues

Starr, J. (2003) *The Coaching Manual*. Edinburgh, Prentice Hall.

Private practice

Fairley, S. and Stout, C. (2004) *Getting Started in Personal and Executive Coaching*. New Jersey, Wiley.

Business issues

Barrow, P. (2001) *The Best-Laid Business Plans: How to Write Them, How to Pitch Them*. London, Virgin Business Guides.
Drake, S. (2001) *Freelancing for Dummies*. New York, Hungry Minds Inc.

Useful contacts and websites

Coaching organisations

A number of professional bodies focus on coaching. The details below are accurate at the time of going to press. Do check their websites for up-to-date information in case of changes.

Association for Coaching

- Has an online register of members and a list of qualified coaches
- The grades of membership are Affiliate, Associate, Member, Fellow, Organisational and Corporate
- Members can use logo
- Has a course recognition system and coach accreditation system
- Runs training and networking events
- http://www.associationforcoaching.com
- info@associationforcoaching.com

European Mentoring and Coaching Council

- Exists to promote good practice and the expectation of good practice in mentoring and coaching across Europe
- Provides a membership forum for all those involved in the wide variety of the applications of coaching and mentoring.
- Members can use logo
- http://www.emccouncil.org

British Psychological Society, Special Group in Coaching Psychology (formerly Coaching Psychology Forum)

- Established 2004 (CPF established 2002)
- BPS members who are in practice or have an interest in coaching psychology
- Open to members of the BPS (non-psychologists can join by becoming BPS Affiliates)
- Full membership open to BPS members with Graduate Basis for Registration
- Has over 1850 members, of whom approximately 50% are chartered psychologists
- Runs CPD events such as workshops and conferences
- Publishes *The Coaching Psychologist* and the *International Coaching Psychology Review*
- http://www.coachingpsychologyforum.org.uk

Association for Professional Executive Coaching and Supervision

- Aims to become the UK's premier professional body for properly qualified executive coaches and those who supervise their work
- Core purpose is to raise the professional standards of executive coaching and the supervision of executive coaching in the workplace
- Membership levels include Accredited Executive Coach and Accredited Supervisor of Executive Coaches
- http://www.apecs.uk.com

Institute of Health Promotion and Education

- Established for over 40 years
- A professional body with a register of members at Associate, Member and Fellow grades
- Runs conferences and publishes an academic journal
- Has members who practise stress management and health coaching
- http://www.ihpe.org.uk
- honsec@ihpe.org.uk

International Coach Federation

- The professional association of personal and business coaches
- Seeks to preserve the integrity of coaching around the globe
- Helps people find the coach most suitable for their needs
- Supports and fosters development of the coaching profession
- Conducts a certification programme
- Holds conferences and other educational events for coaches
- The largest non-profit professional association worldwide of personal and business coaches with more than 6000 members and 145 chapters in 30 countries
- http://www.coachfederation.org

International Association of Coaches

- Officially launched March 11, 2003 as a non-profit entity in the state of New Mexico
- Over 8000 members
- Mission is to further the interests of coaching clients worldwide
- Has a rigorous and objective coach testing and certification procedure
- Membership is currently free
- Members can use IAC logo
- Intention is to be a separate entity responsible for managing the certification process of the "15 Proficiencies"
- http://www.certifiedcoach.org

Counselling and psychotherapy organisations for referrals

British Association for Counselling and Psychotherapy
BACP House, 35–37 Albert Street, Rugby, Warwickshire
CV21 2SG, UK
bacp@bacp.co.uk
http://www.bacp.co.uk
The BACP have now set up a coaching forum group.

United Kingdom Register of Counsellors
BACP House, 35–37 Albert Street, Rugby, Warwickshire
CV21 2SG, UK
Tel: 0870 443 5232
Fax: 0870 443 5161
ukrc@bacp.co.uk
http://www.ukrconline.org.uk/register.html

United Kingdom Council for Psychotherapy
167–169 Great Portland Street, London W1W 5PF, UK
Tel: 020 7436 3002
Fax: 020 7436 3013
ukcp@psychotherapy.org.uk
http://www.psychotherapy.org.uk

Training courses

Centre for Coaching
156 Westcombe Hill, London SE3 7DH, UK
Tel: 020 8293 4334
Fax: 020 8293 4114
admin@centreforcoaching.com
http://www.centreforcoaching.com

The Coaching and Mentoring Network
http://www.coachingnetwork.org.uk

Chartered Institute of Personnel and Development (CIPD)
CIPD House, Camp Road, London SW19 4UX, UK
http://www.cipd.co.uk

Stephen Palmer Partnership Ltd
PO Box 438, Harpenden, Herts AL5 4WY, UK
Tel/Fax: 01582 712161
kate_thomas@btinternet.com
http://www.stephenpalmerpartnership.com

Government organisations

Data Protection Registrar
Wycliffe House, Water Lane, Wilmslow, Cheshire SK9 5AF,
UK
http://www.dataprotection.gov.uk
http://www.disability.gov.uk

Customs and Excise Central Office
London Central Office, Berkeley House, 304 Regents Park
Road, Finchley, London N3 2JY, UK
Tel: 020 7865 4400
Fax: 020 8346 9154
http://www.hmce.gov.uk

Inland Revenue
http://www.inlandrevenue.gov.uk

Insurance Company

SMG
SMG House, 31 Clarendon Road, Leeds, UK
Tel: 0113 294 4000
http://www.smg-professional-risks.co.uk

Business advice

Business Link
http://www.businesslink.gov.uk

Training in setting up in private practice

Centre for Coaching
156 Westcombe Hill, London SE3 7DH, UK
Tel: 020 8293 4334
Fax: 020 8293 4114
admin@centreforcoaching.com
http://www.centreforcoaching.com

Internet providers

Easyspace
One of many internet providers. You can purchase your
domain name and host your website on their servers.
http://www.easyspace.com

Bizland
An internet provider which also provides relatively easy-to-
use free templates to design your website. In addition you can
purchase your domain name.
http://www.bizland.com

FreeWeb
Provides free hosting, free domain and website templates.
http://www.freewebs.com

Accountancy professional bodies

The Institute of Chartered Accountants in England and Wales
The institute is the largest professional accountancy body in
Europe, with over 118,000 members. Its chartered
accountancy qualification is recognised internationally.
Chartered Accountants' Hall, PO Box 433, London EC2P 2BJ,
UK
Tel: 020 7920 8100
Fax: 020 7920 8547
http://www.icaew.co.uk

The Institute of Chartered Accountants in Scotland
Head Office, CA House, 21 Haymarket Yards, Edinburgh
EH12 5BH, UK
Tel: 0131 347 0100
Fax: 0131 347 0105
enquiries@icas.org.uk
http://www.icas.org.uk

Ulster Society of Chartered Accountants
The Secretary, CA House, 87–89 Pembroke Road, Dublin 4,
Eire
Tel: +353 1 668 0400
Fax: +353 1 668 5685
ca@icai.ie.
http://www.icai.ie
Belfast office: 11 Donegall Square South, Belfast BT1 5JE,
UK
Tel: 02890 321600
Fax: 02890 230071

Association of Chartered Certified Accountants (ACCA)
The largest global professional accountancy body
64 Finnieston Square, Glasgow G3 8DT, UK
General enquiries: info@accaglobal.com
Student enquiries: students@accaglobal.com
Member enquiries: members@accaglobal.com
http://www.acca.co.uk
Tel: 0141 582 2000
Fax: 0141 582 2222

The Chartered Institute of Public Finance and Accountancy
3 Robert Street, London WC2N 6RL, UK
Tel: 020 7543 5600
Fax: 020 7543 5700
http://www.cipfa.org.uk

The Chartered Institute of Management Accountants
26 Chapter Street, London SW1P 4NP, UK
Tel: 020 7663 5441
Fax: 020 7663 5442
http://www.cimaglobal.com/

Institute of Financial Accountants
Burford House, 44 London Road, Sevenoaks, Kent TN13 1AS,
UK
Tel: 01732 458080
Fax: 01732 455848
mail@ifa.org.uk
http://www.ifa.org.uk

Association of International Accountants
South Bank Building, Kingsway, Team Valley, Newcastle
upon Tyne NE11 0JS, UK
Tel: 0191 482 4409
Fax: 0191 482 5578
aia@aia.org.uk
http://www.aia.org.uk

Book-keeping professional bodies

The Institute of Certified Book-Keepers
12 St James' Square, London SW1Y 4RB, UK
Tel: 0845 060 2345
info@book-keepers.org

International Association of Book-Keepers
Burford House, 44 London Road, Sevenoaks, Kent TN13 1AS,
UK
Tel: 01732 467123
Fax: 01732 455848
http://www.iab.org.uk

The Chartered Institute of Taxation
The leading UK body which focusses on taxation.
12 Upper Belgrave Street, London SW1X 8BB, UK
Tel: 020 7235 9381
Fax: 020 7235 2562
post@tax.org.uk
http://www.tax.org.uk

Index